IMAGES
of America

THE OREGON AIR NATIONAL GUARD

The Redhawk insignia first appeared on the Lockheed F-5 Photo Lightning reconnaissance aircraft and the uniform jackets of the men of the 35th Photographic Reconnaissance Squadron (PRS) in 1944 in the China-Burma-India theater of operations during World War II. The 35th PRS was formed from the 123rd Observation Squadron of the Oregon Air National Guard (ORANG) in 1943. A common Oregon bird of prey, the red-tailed hawk was remembered in this emblem. Twin tails were evocative of the twin-boomed F-5 aircraft the unit flew, and the camera was symbolic of the photographic reconnaissance mission of the squadron. The Redhawk insignia was retained after World War II when the 35th once again became the 123rd and is depicted in a modified form today on the F-15 aircraft and patches of the ORANG's 123rd Fighter Squadron. (Courtesy of the 142nd Fighter Wing History Archives.)

On the Cover: A pair of Convair F-102 Delta Daggers of the 123rd Fighter Interceptor Squadron, ORANG, thunder past scenic Mount Hood in the late 1960s. The ORANG flew this interceptor aircraft from Portland Air Base between 1966 and 1971. (Courtesy of the 142nd Fighter Wing History Archives.)

IMAGES
of America

THE OREGON AIR NATIONAL GUARD

Terrence G. Popravak Jr.
and Sean M. Popravak

ARCADIA
PUBLISHING

ISBN 978-0-7385-9312-8

Published by Arcadia Publishing
Charleston, South Carolina

Printed in the United States of America

Library of Congress Control Number: 2011938565

For all general information, please contact Arcadia Publishing:
Telephone 843-853-2070
Fax 843-853-0044
E-mail sales@arcadiapublishing.com
For customer service and orders:
Toll-Free 1-888-313-2665

Visit us on the Internet at www.arcadiapublishing.com

To the ORANG's founder, Brig. Gen. G. Robert Dodson, and to the men and women of the Oregon Air National Guard, past, present, and future.

Publisher's Note: Publishing community standards are used herein for the abbreviation of military rank, which may vary from service-specific abbreviations.

Contents

FOREWORD

As war clouds were forming in the early 1940s, the Oregon National Guard announced that it was organizing its first aviation unit. On April 18, 1941, I was privileged to step forward with 116 other carefully selected young men to be sworn in and form the 123rd Observation Squadron under the command of Maj. G. Robert Dodson.

We were quickly issued uniforms and equipment to begin accelerated training and drills at the Swan Island Municipal Airport in Portland. On September 15, 1941, we were called to active service and were soon moved to Gray Field, Fort Lewis, Washington. There, we joined with the 116th Observation Squadron from the Washington National Guard to form the 70th Observation Group.

As training progressed, a number of men elected to go to air cadet schools for pilots, navigators, bombardiers, and observers. Many others were sent to various military technical schools to train as air mechanics, radio operators, ordnance specialists, and for other positions. I was sent to the School of Aviation Medicine in Texas and became a certified flight surgeon's assistant.

Several men of the 123rd (including me) were transferred to other newly formed squadrons being added to the 70th Group. Upon my return from school, I was transferred to 70th Group Headquarters and promoted accordingly.

In 1943, the renamed 123rd Photo Reconnaissance Squadron was moved to California and redesignated the 35th Photo Reconnaissance Squadron. Late in 1944, the 70th Group was dissolved, and the 35th was sent to the China-Burma-India theater of operations to fly reconnaissance missions in China with the 14th Air Force.

Personnel of the original unit served in every combat theater of operations in World War II. Regrettably, a few of our men did not come home. A number of the original members were awarded decorations signifying various outstanding performances in the service to their country.

After the war, the Oregon Air National Guard was reorganized to become one of the nation's outstanding Air Guards. The men and women of today's Oregon Air Guard strive diligently to continually improve on the high standards of excellence that have been established before them.

There are very few original members left. We are proud to have served, and we are proud of the men and women now serving.

—T/Sgt Fred C. Parish
Army Air Corps
World War II

ACKNOWLEDGMENTS

We thank the following persons and organizations who made this work possible. We first thank the 142nd Fighter Wing commander, Col. Michael Stencel, and the Wing Public Affairs officer, Maj. Melinda Lepore, for allowing us access to the wing's historical archives, which provided much of the information and most of the images for this book; unless otherwise noted, all images appear courtesy of the 142nd Fighter Wing Historical Archives. We thank many veterans and current ORANG members whom we interviewed and/or who contributed images and stories, including but not limited to Fred Parish, Fred Hill, Glen Curry, John Pear, John Donis, William Stevenson, H. Allen Larsen, Jack Barden, Jack Klein, Ernie Wakehouse, Gene Thomas, Brad Newell, Michael Brown, Gene Hellickson, Greg James, Sterling Barrow, Ron Edwards, Armand LaBelle, Bill Avolio, Col. Michael Bieniewicz, C.M.Sgt. Patrick Tracy, C.M.Sgt. John Rasmussen, and T.Sgt. John Hughel. Regards to Lt. Col. Alisha Hamel, Oregon Military Department, and Tracy Thoennes, curator, Oregon Military Museum, for their historical help. Thanks to Aileen Garra-Lim, Steve Blake, and 1st Lt. Daniel Jackson, who helped with 35th PRS veteran connections. Appreciation to Lynne Gifford for permitting us to share photographs from her father, 35th PRS veteran Chester Krejci. We thank Brig. Gen. Kennard Wiggins (Retired) of the Delaware Air National Guard for his inspiring aviation historical work and counsel. We appreciate history advice and assistance from air defense guru Marty Isham and US Air Force Global Strike Command historian Yancey Mailes. Thanks also to Northwest aviation enthusiasts and photographers Ron Olsen and Paul Carter. International thanks to ppłk. dypl. (Lt. Col.) Maciej Kłótka in Poland. Our thanks go also to Carol Alhadeff at Jantzen, LLC, and Aaron Grossman of the Portland Trail Blazers. Fond remembrance in thanks to S.M.Sgt John R. "Jack" Gallant, ORANG veteran and neighbor, and his family, through whom the author was first introduced to the ORANG in the F-101 era. Thanks to Donna Libert, our editor at Arcadia, for her good help in seeing this project through to fruition. Special thanks to Terrence Sr. and Helen Popravak for childhood library trips that captured the lure of aviation. Heartfelt thanks to Edelina Popravak and Nathan Popravak for allowing Terrence Jr. time away from family to pursue this work. And last but not least, thanks to our Savior Jesus Christ for His mercy, grace, and inspiration.

—Terrence G. Popravak Jr. and Sean M. Popravak
Vancouver, Washington

Introduction

The American spirit is one that embodies initiative to recognize a need and to design and implement a solution to satisfy it. So it was in 1941, with airpower advocates like Oregonian G. Robert Dodson, the first commander of the Oregon National Guard's 123rd Observation Squadron, the state's first military aviation unit.

Following World War II, an Air National Guard was organized with the abundant combat-experienced personnel and equipment on hand. During the Cold War, the mission of many Air National Guard (ANG) units was shaped by growing requirements for air defense as the Soviets developed long-range bombers and nuclear weapons. The Korean War led to a significant expansion of the air defense mission, in which the Air National Guard, including the ORANG, played a critical role.

The ORANG commenced air defense operations with the propeller-driven F-51 Mustang and then with jets. Since the late 1950s, the ORANG has had fighters on air defense alert in the Pacific Northwest and provides this Aerospace Control Alert capability today, 24 hours a day, seven days a week, 365 days a year.

But fighter aircraft, with air and ground crews that fly, fix, fuel, and feed them, are but one part of an effective air defense system. From its early days, the ORANG also provided air surveillance and control with ground-based radars and command, control, and communications centers.

Regularly, the ORANG responds to the urgent needs of Oregonians, from flood to forest fire. These citizen airmen also help their local communities in any number of less urgent but important roles, from toy and food drives for the needy to the annual Camp Rosenbaum Youth Camp to air shows that highlight the contributions of airpower to the public.

Periodically, the ORANG responds to the nation's call, as it first did during the Korean War. During the height of the Cold War, Oregon Guardsmen even deployed to central Europe to help provide North Atlantic Treaty Organization (NATO) forces an essential air defense alert capability. Many other deployments have followed in state, out of state, and around the world.

Through all these postwar years, the continuity of the air defense mission is a resounding theme for the ORANG. But air defense is a lot like insurance: no one thinks much about it until one needs it. And like insurance, if one does not have it, one might unduly suffer. On the eve of September 11, 2001, there were but 14 fighters on alert duty across the United States—two of those alert aircraft belonged to the ORANG.

Today, there are but a few fighter units dedicated to homeland air defense, and each is also tasked with additional global expeditionary responsibilities. These air defense units, all Air National Guard, are the core excellence of the nation's remaining air defense expertise. Oregon's sky sentinels maintain their vigil for Oregon, the Pacific Northwest, and the United States. Hopefully, the powers that be will also continue to provide the ORANG and the other remaining members of the strategic air defense community with the resources they need to assure our air sovereignty and aerospace control in an uncertain, sometimes hostile world.

One

1940s

Birth, War, and Rebirth

Following the August 1940 authorization to form the Oregon National Guard's first aviation unit, recruitment began in March 1941. The 123rd commenced operations at Swan Island Airport in Portland with two officers, 108 enlisted men, and two aircraft, a BC-1A and an O-46A.

On September 15, 1941, the squadron was called to active federal service, and it soon moved to Gray Field, Washington, where it received the O-47 aircraft. On December 7, 1941, the 123rd flew one of the first wartime missions from a US base and subsequently patrolled the Pacific Northwest coast. Additionally, the squadron supported ground forces training at Fort Lewis and the Yakima Range.

Reflecting aerial reconnaissance wartime experience and lessons learned from the North African campaign, in March 1943, the 123rd was redesignated as a reconnaissance squadron. In August 1943, it became the 35th Photo Reconnaissance Squadron (PRS). Not all 123rd personnel served with the 35th PRS, however. Most were already with other units in the Army Air Forces' gigantic buildup and served worldwide.

In April 1944, the squadron sailed for the Far East, reaching India in June 1944. There, it assembled, organized, and then flew over the Himalayas into China. From September 1944 to August 1945, the unit flew the F-5 reconnaissance variant of the P-38 Lightning in the China-Burma-India theater with 14th Air Force, the famous Flying Tigers. The 35th inactivated after the war on November 7, 1945, at Camp Kilmer, New Jersey. The squadron received credit for participation in seven World War II campaigns.

Scant months later, the 35th PRS was reactivated, redesignated as the 123rd Fighter Squadron, and allocated to the Oregon National Guard, effective June 26, 1946. Postwar growth came when the 142nd Fighter Group (FG) was allocated to Oregon on May 24, 1946. Both organizations were stationed at Portland Air Base. In early 1947, the first P-51s arrived, joining two AT-6 trainers on hand.

Columbia River flooding disrupted many lives in 1948 and inundated the ORANG's home. The planned summer encampment was cancelled as efforts focused on cleanup and rebuilding. But the ORANG bounced back quickly, and by the end of the decade, it was again ready to answer the call.

G. Robert Dodson, Oregonian and top executive of the Jantzen Knitting Mills, Inc., began his military career in 1938. He played a prominent role in the creation of the Oregon National Guard's first aviation unit, the 123rd Observation Squadron, and became the unit's first commander. He is pictured here on the wing of the 123rd's North American BC-1A, the unit's first aircraft, received in May 1941.

From February 1941 to September 1941, Maj. Carlisle Ferris (right) was the first regular Air Corps instructor assigned to help organize the Oregon National Guard's air squadron and obtain its federal recognition. The father of famous aviation artist Keith Ferris, he is shown here at Swan Island Airport with Major Dodson. (Courtesy of Fred Parish.)

The Oregon National Guard Armory in Portland on Northwest Eleventh Avenue was used for recruiting squadron members and was where the first personnel of the 123rd received their physical exams and swore their oaths of enlistment prior to joining the squadron. The building still exists today as the Gerding Theater at the Armory.

Officers and men of the Oregon National Guard's 123rd Observation Squadron assembled with the unit's O-46A and BC-1A aircraft for this picture in the summer of 1941 at Swan Island Airport. (Courtesy of John Donis.)

Members of the 123rd Observation Squadron pose in front of the unit's second aircraft, a Douglas O-46A, at Swan Island Airport in the summer of 1941 while still on National Guard duty status. From left to right are Robert Davis, C. Barclay Peterson, John Donis, Owen Bottler, and Clarence Allesina. (Courtesy of John Donis.)

Pay day! Oregon's first aviation Guardsmen line up at the Swan Island Airport to receive their drill pay during the brief period between when the unit was formed and when it was activated for federal service. From left to right are (hand in pocket) Roderick Buchanan, Jack Shaylor, (possibly) Clifford Shaffer, Dean Altman, (receiving pay) Burchill Shelton or John Flavin, and (handing out pay) Robert Burkholder. The others are unidentified.

Early on September 25, 1941, the squadron met for breakfast at Hilaire's Restaurant on Southwest Washington Street in downtown Portland, then mustered and marched with a band and police escort down to Union Station to entrain for Gray Field, Washington. Here, the unit marches, led by 1st Sgt. John O'Keefe, with the famous Hoyt Hotel in the background.

When the 123rd was mobilized and sent to Gray Army Airfield in September 1941, it brought along its two aircraft. Here, in the shadow of majestic Mount Rainier, the O-46, known as "Old Awful" to some and now wearing camouflage paint, runs up its engine whilst the BC-1A sits silently in the foreground.

Shortly after arriving at Gray Field, the squadron began to operate the portly North American O-47 observation aircraft. The new aircraft came from the 116th Observation Squadron, a Washington National Guard unit also mobilized for federal service and stationed at Gray Field. A 123rd aircrew in an O-47 spotted a Japanese submarine off the mouth of the Columbia River on December 24, 1941.

A tent used by the photography section of the 123rd as an office was located on the side of a Gray Field hangar. It is the second tent from the left in this c. 1942 view. The objects on the board to the right of the 123rd's tent door are not bulletins but photographic prints drying in the sunlight.

Aerial photography was an integral part of the observation mission. Here S.Sgt. Roy Wolford stands outside the 123rd photography section in his flying attire holding a Fairchild K-3B aerial camera, which was invented in the 1920s and was a forerunner of wartime cameras like the K-17. The handles and viewfinder on top indicate it will be used for handheld and not aircraft-mounted operations.

Pvt. Fred Parish, the 123rd's medic, stands next to an ambulance, which appears to be a Dodge 1/2-ton WC9 type, at Fort Lewis, near Gray Field, in 1942. (Courtesy of Fred Parish.)

Fred Hill initially joined the 186th Infantry, Oregon National Guard, in 1940. He was mobilized and stationed with his unit at Fort Lewis and later became the first new member to join the 123rd Observation Squadron after the squadron left Portland and moved to Gray Field. Pictured here as a corporal in September 1942, his uniform bears the Army Air Corps patch (left shoulder), evocative of an aircraft propeller in motion. (Courtesy of Fred Hill.)

After Pearl Harbor, the 123rd flew patrols off the west coast, searching for signs of any enemy activity. The squadron periodically deployed aircraft to Moon Island Airport, Washington, a bare base just west of Hoquiam. The Army lengthened its runway in 1942 and used it for these offshore patrols. Squadron personnel billeted in hotels in town. Here, 123rd members are busy on the Moon Island flight line near a Stinson L-1A Vigilant observation plane.

At the Moon Island Airport in 1942, a woman in a mobile food truck serves the 123rd. All personnel in this view are unidentified, though the three men to the left are all aircrew. Of note, the near corner of the shack to the right had a rudimentary kitchen, and a 123rd cook was detailed to serve there in support of operations.

The 123rd celebrated its first anniversary on active duty in September 1942 with a variety of activities in Hoquiam, Washington. Here, squadron members play a baseball game. From left to right behind the unidentified batter in the foreground are Leo Amedio, Hugo Besocke, unidentified, Burch Shelton (white shirt), Fred Parish, and additional unidentified men. (Courtesy of Fred Parish.)

The squadron held a party in the evening at a Hoquiam hotel to celebrate its first anniversary. Hamming it up at the microphone is Major Dodson's successor and the squadron's second commander, Capt. Wallace O'Daniels (left), and M.Sgt. Clarence Allesina.

As the Army increased in size, the 123rd assisted with the training of new formations. Here, O-47s conduct a mock attack on troops still wearing the World War I–style helmet.

Photographer S.Sgt. Roy Wolford looks back from the middle seat of an O-47. From here, he could lower himself into the belly of the aircraft to tend to the aerial cameras it carried.

Aircraft and crews of the 123rd were sent to support Army training activities in Yakima, Washington, during late 1942 to the early 1943. The facilities were primitive; however, this O-47 takes advantage of the relative warmth of a cover over its engine.

Here, a 123rd ground crew in Yakima copes with the difficult winter weather while performing open-air maintenance on an O-47 engine. The men are unidentified, except for (possibly) Jack Shaylor on the far right, next to the engine cowling.

Of the original 123rd Observation Squadron members, 13 served with the 35th PRS in China. Ten of these Oregon Guardsmen are pictured here at Chanyi. They are, from left to right, (first row) John Flavin, John Buckner, Kenneth Miller, and Jack Shaylor; (second row) Harry Bachman, Roy Wolford, Charles Estes, Harvey Lounsbury, Lorne Restau, and Cyrus Dolph.

Unidentified mechanics of the 35th PRS stand with one of the squadron's Lockheed F-5E Photo Lightning reconnaissance aircraft. It was in China that the distinctive Redhawk insignia first appeared, as seen on the nose of this aircraft.

Capt. Joe Sipper (from Detroit) walks near the runway as a Lockheed F-5 buzzes the airfield at Chihkiang. The 35th PRS operated a detachment of F-5s at this airfield from October 19, 1944, until September 1, 1945. (Courtesy of Chester Krejci family.)

This image illustrates why the 35th PRS went to war—to obtain aerial photography of vital targets behind enemy lines. This print from an actual combat mission has been processed and annotated by photograph interpreters to show significant features and Japanese installations and equipment at Samah Beach, located on the south side of Hainan Island, China. (Courtesy of H. Allen Larsen.)

The 35th PRS warmly received a USO troupe led by entertainer Jinx Falkenburg and actor Pat O'Brien in late 1944. Here, Jinx and Pat engage the troops from a modest stage at Chanyi, China, where the 35th PRS established its headquarters in September 1944. This troupe was well regarded, as it traveled 12,000 miles over a two-month schedule, putting up 84 performances, excluding hospital shows, though it was only scheduled for 54 shows.

Jinx and the troupe also visited the 35th squadron and shared a meal with the Redhawks. Here, she chats with squadron members, including, from left to right, an unidentified officer, 1st Sgt. John Flavin, and Jack Shaylor. Note the Redhawk emblem on the back wall.

American units and servicemen overseas occasionally adopted a local youth, sometimes an orphan, to clean their quarters or wash their laundry. This photograph shows members of the 35th PRS at Chanyi with one possible such adoptee, a Chinese boy in a custom uniform. From left to right are (first row) unidentified, unidentified boy, and unidentified; (second row) Harry Bachman and Roy Wolford.

T.Sgt. Roy Riehl in China holds up a January 4, 1945, copy of the *CBI Roundup*, a popular military newspaper in the China-Burma-India theater of operations.

The cost of war is illustrated in the destruction of a $97,147 Lockheed F-5 aircraft (the average cost for a P-38 in 1944). This image may be of the takeoff mishap of 35th PRS pilot Jim Kerr at Chanyi; fortunately, he survived. An F-5 carried a pair of larger 300-gallon drop tanks for extra-long-range missions (versus 165-gallon tanks). With the larger and heavier tanks, an F-5 quickly consumed an unimproved 5,000-foot Chinese runway on takeoff with little or no room to spare.

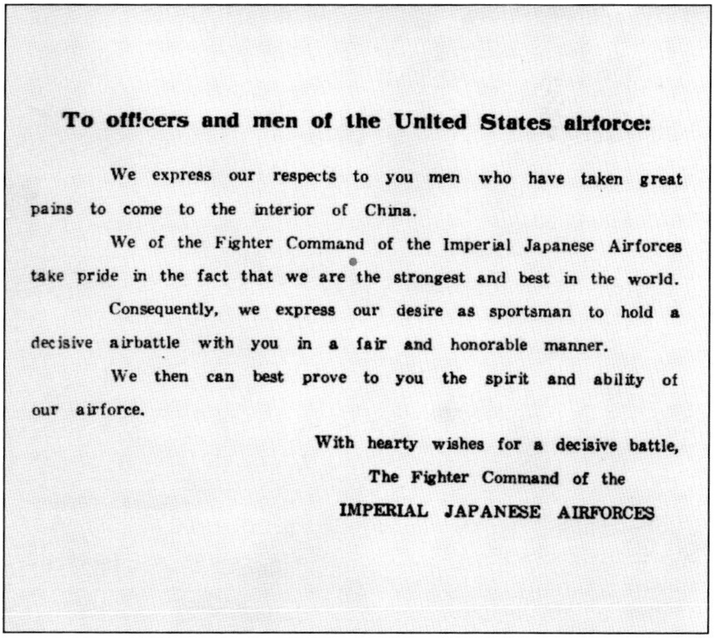

To officers and men of the United States airforce:

We express our respects to you men who have taken great pains to come to the interior of China.

We of the Fighter Command of the Imperial Japanese Airforces take pride in the fact that we are the strongest and best in the world.

Consequently, we express our desire as sportsman to hold a decisive airbattle with you in a fair and honorable manner.

We then can best prove to you the spirit and ability of our airforce.

With hearty wishes for a decisive battle,
The Fighter Command of the
IMPERIAL JAPANESE AIRFORCES

Propaganda leaflets are common devices in wartime psychological operations. This is an example of a Japanese calling card that 35th PRS members encountered in China.

Two unidentified officers stand next to another 35th PRS F-5 adorned with a Redhawk. The aircraft has many mission symbols painted on it, including a mountain for the initial deployment into theater over the Himalayas, over 60 reconnaissance missions, and, curiously, a bomb symbol. There is a report of an unauthorized combat mission flown by the squadron employing napalm against Japanese troops—the unit was quickly orders by headquarters to stick to photographic reconnaissance. (Courtesy of Chester Krejci family.)

At the end of World War II, Japanese forces surrendered to their allied counterparts in each part of the Pacific. Two 123rd veterans, John Donis (110th Tactical Reconnaissance Squadron) and Fred Hill (17th Reconnaissance Squadron) witnessed such an event on August 19, 1945, at Ie Shima, located near Okinawa, Japan. Here, at Ie Shima, a Japanese surrender delegation prepares to board a C-54 bound for Manila to meet with General MacArthur. (Courtesy of John Donis.)

In China, the surrender of Japanese forces was arranged via an official delegation that flew to Chihkiang Airfield on August 21, 1945, where a flight of the 35th PRS was deployed. Squadron members witnessed the arrival of the surrender delegation aboard a Japanese Ki-57 Topsy (transport version of Ki-21 Sally bomber), on its way to meet with Chinese military leaders. (Courtesy of Chester Krejci Family.)

A pair of Oregon National Guard P-51 Mustangs plies the Northwest skies in this c. 1947 view. Note the large National Guard buzz number painted on top of the right wing of the closest aircraft, a handy visual identification reference, especially for any low-flying aircraft over populated areas.

A row of five Oregon National Guard Mustangs rests on a parking ramp in this image, captured around 1947. The Oregon National Guard received its first P-51 Mustang fighters in early 1947. At the time, the organization had two AT-6 trainers on hand. The initial plan was to equip the Oregon National Guard with 25 P-51s, two AT-6s, three A-26s, one C-47, and two L-5s.

The variety in the Oregon National Guard's initial postwar aircraft is shown in this view from the second level in the main maintenance hangar. Seen from left to right are an AT-6 trainer, a C-47 transport, and a P-51 fighter, with the nose of an A-26 bomber in the bottom right.

Guardsmen stand by one of the unit's A-26 aircraft in this late 1940s picture. From left to right are ? Morris, unidentified, ? Ward, unidentified, Victor Strunik, Dan Rouden, unidentified, and Paul Wagner. The bomber's nose art represents its target towing duty. On June 11, 1948, the US Air Force (USAF) instituted a new aircraft designation system. The A for Attack designation was dropped, and Douglas A-26 Invader aircraft were redesignated B-26.

An Oregon mechanic, possibly Sgt. ? Underdall, works on the engine of a 123rd Fighter Squadron P-51 Mustang in the maintenance hangar at Portland Air Base in this post–World War II view.

A neat and orderly ORANG base supply office is shown in this 1948 view. It was located in the front of the Portland Air Base supply warehouse. From left to right are noncommissioned officers (NCOs) Jim Schoonmaker Sr. (assistant to the supply officer), supply clerks Harry Schoonmaker and Luther Leonard, and Richard Perrigo, who managed the base aviation fuel system.

The Oregon National Guard's early postwar aviation recruiting was conducted in many creative ways. In 1947, a P-51 Mustang was emplaced in the bargain basement of Portland's downtown Meier & Frank Department Store, the largest department store in Oregon. Twenty-five aircraft mechanics and store maintenance personnel worked together using assorted jacks and dollies to manhandle the aircraft into place atop a special display frame (the engine was removed to reduce weight).

Here, an Oregon Air Guard P-51 Mustang, bedecked with roses, took part in Portland's famous Rose Festival in 1947. This was another creative way to advertise aviation opportunities with the Oregon National Guard.

Portland's F-51s attracted other flowers, too. Maj. Carl Brose, 123rd Flight Squadron operations officer, talks with his hands to explain the flying business to an unidentified attentive young lady as supply officer Gordon Gemmel (left) and line chief M.Sgt. William Harlow pay attention to her. She wears a Jantzen swimsuit (bearing the Diving Girl logo) of a style called "Too Sweet," which was part of the company's 1949 swim line and had a retail price of $12.95.

Tragedy struck Portland in May and June 1948, when the Columbia River breached boundaries at several locations in the region, causing extensive flooding, damage, and loss of life. Portland Air Base was also flooded in the catastrophe. Here, an Oregon B-26 is seen mostly underwater in the base's main hangar. The aircraft was ruined and never flew again.

Two

1950s

Cold War and Hot

The call to duty was not long in coming. After the Korean War began in June 1950, the ORANG contributed to the sudden requirement for additional F-51 Mustang fighters needed for service in Korea. Oregon pilots flew several F-51s to California, where they were loaded on a carrier and rushed to the Far East.

Late in 1950, elements of the ORANG mobilized in response to the war. The first to be called was the 1810th Engineer Aviation Company. After that, nine fighter pilots were individually mobilized from the 123rd Fighter Squadron, and they flew over 1,000 combat missions in Korea. Remaining elements of the 142nd Fighter Group were also activated for 21 months, served in place at Portland, and received an infusion of active-duty personnel, even as some Air Guardsmen were detailed elsewhere to serve, like in World War II. Thus, the 142nd provided air defense in the region and performed a valuable operational training role.

Last but not least, in May 1951, the 142nd Aircraft Control and Warning Squadron was activated and then transported by ship to Alaska. The squadron established several radar sites along the Bering Sea coastline opposite the Soviet Union. They bolstered ground radar coverage and maintained a lonely vigil in remote areas against the emerging Soviet nuclear bomber threat.

With the end of the Korean War, air defense became the ORANG's primary mission, and the 142nd Fighter Group remained on the front lines of continental air defense through the Cold War years. This mission led to the operation of several types of fighter interceptor aircraft. With these interceptors, the ORANG firmly established its air defense credentials. In the late 1950s, the 142nd began standing air defense alert, and it continues to do so to this day.

Another development of the decade that continues today is the service of women in the ORANG. In March 1958, 1st Lt. Faith Hunsdon became the first woman to join Oregon's Air Guard.

ORANG pilot 1st Lt. Ernie Wakehouse stands by an armed F-51 Mustang during the Korean War. After his activation, he flew 100 combat missions in Korea from September to December 1951 with the 39th Fighter Squadron. Nine ORANG pilots went to Korea and flew 1,051 missions, claimed one enemy aircraft destroyed, dropped 1,056 bombs, fired 3,715 rockets, dropped 456 Napalm bombs, and fired 1,194,000 rounds of .50-caliber machine gun cartridges. (Courtesy of Gene Thomas.)

While the 123rd Fighter Squadron was not deployed, it was brought into federal service from February 1951 to until December 1952 at Portland Air Base. During this period, the unit received new pilots and personnel and served a valuable air defense and operational training role. Here, F-51Ds bearing the Redhawk emblem rest on the ramp at Portland.

During the latter period of its active-duty service, the 123rd received the North American F-86F Sabre jet fighter, the first jet fighter flown by Oregon Air Guardsmen. In this image, a 123rd F-86F-1-NA plies the skies bearing the Redhawk emblem. The Air Force (AF) retained these late-model Sabres when the 123rd completed its active-duty tour and was returned to the state of Oregon. (Courtesy of Marty Isham.)

This October 1953 view of Portland's ramp shows the transition from propellers to jets. For a brief period, the Oregon ANG was to convert to the Republic F-84 Thunderjet. Personnel trained for it, and the unit received one example before higher headquarters changed plans. Here, F-84B 45-59554, T-6s, and a T-33 share the ramp with Mustangs. This F-84B is reportedly in storage today at the Pima Air Museum in Arizona. (Courtesy of Marty Isham.)

The next aircraft the ORANG converted to was the early-model F-86A Sabre, its first jet combat aircraft as an Air Guard formation. It operated the Sabre from September 1953 until late in 1955. The new Sabres pictured occupy the Portland ramp, with the nose of a departing Mustang on the right edge of the photograph.

M.Sgt. Fred Boero works on an ORANG F-86A in the hangar at Portland in this mid-1950s view. Note that the platform he is standing on belongs to the active-duty 503rd Air Defense Group's Material Squadron, a sign of some of the cooperation between the Guard, Reserve, and active-duty Air Force units at Portland Air Base.

Col. Gordon Doolittle leads a group of Oregon Air Guardsmen down Southwest Fifth Avenue during the Armed Forces Day Parade in Portland in May 1954.

The ORANG participated in the 1955 Earl T. Ricks Memorial Trophy jet air race between Ontario, California, and Detroit, Michigan. Lt. Col. Staryl Austin flew his "Gal-O-My Dreams," which is shown being serviced at Buckley Field, Colorado, during the race, July 2, 1955. Maj. Walt Williams gives Lieutenant Colonel Austin a weather update while Capt. Chuck Toynbee supervises the removal of drop tanks. The other men at the aircraft are unidentified.

Sabre days were numbered in Oregon when the Lockheed F-94B appeared in late 1955. Here, a simply marked F-94 sits between an F-86 and a T-33 with colorful ORANG markings. The F-94B was the ORANG's last gun-only aircraft before the arrival of fighters with air-to-air rocket and missile armament. The F-94B was armed with four .50-caliber machine guns mounted in the lower part of the nose.

A variety of aircraft received attention in the main hangar at Portland. In this c. 1956–1957 image, an ORANG C-47 and TB-25 lie in the shadows while an AF Reserve Beech AT-11 sits in the doorway.

The ORANG's C-47 served from 1947 to 1966. This September 1954 view shows it after white paint was applied to the top of the fuselage to help with cooling the interior. This aircraft provided humanitarian assistance in June 1960, when four polio patients were returned to their Oregon homes from treatment in California after commercial aircraft were unable to accommodate power requirements for the patients' respirators.

The ORANG operated a Beech C-45H Expeditor during the 1950s. The C-45 was a remanufactured Beech AT-7/AT-11 trainer whose airframe was brought to zero time; thus, it was given a 1952 serial number. It was used for a variety of support missions from transport to cargo, liaison, and administrative tasks.

Brig. Gen. G. Robert Dodson disembarks from Oregon's C-45H in this July 1955 picture. Even with his leadership and administrative duties as the commander of the ORANG, he flew when he could. He became ill while at the 1958 summer camp at Gowen Field, Idaho, and passed away in December 1958 at age 54. A Portland native, Brigadier General Dodson attended Washington High School and the University of Oregon.

In this view, F-94B fighter interceptors undergo maintenance in the new ORANG hangar. Note the presence of a sole T-33A and C-45 amidst nine F-94Bs. The F-94s sport a late modification to boost the aircraft's firepower with two additional .50-caliber machine guns in a pod mounted on the leading edge of each wing, which gave the F-94B a total of eight .50-cal machine guns.

The ORANG's Lloyd Buckley, who ran the sheet metal shop, invented a modification for several of its auxiliary power units, fitting them with an extending arm to keep the electrical cable off the ground. One is shown here hooked up to a 123rd Fighter Interceptor Squadron (FIS) F-94B. This feature enabled the ground crews to save the time previously needed to coil up the cables and hang them on the cart.

The ORANG operated a North American TB-25K Mitchell from December 1955 to December 1957 for the training of F-94 radar observers. Here, M.Sgt. Ray Dahm is running up the aircraft's engines whilst M.Sgt. Dave McKinnon stands fireguard. They were both flight engineers and had approximately 2,500 and 3,500 flight hours, respectively.

Crew chief T.Sgt. Kenneth Powers helps a young woman, probably Myrna Gail Johnson, Miss Air Fair 1956 for the air show at Portland Air Base, in viewing a T-33 jet trainer in this July 1956 photograph. It was no small feat for this winsome visitor to climb up and down the crew ladder and enter and exit the cockpit wearing high heels.

Air Guardsmen volunteered to help advertise opportunities at the 1956 Portland Homeshow; from left to right are M.Sgt. John Nielson, Capt. Earl Ellis, and CWO3 Darl Jordan. Soon thereafter, the US Air Force decided to eliminate its warrant officer ranks and increase the highest rank in the NCO corps from master sergeant to chief master sergeant, a change established in 1958. Warrant officers already in the service continued to serve until they retired.

A clean Northrop F-89H Scorpion fighter interceptor in natural metal finish sits in the sun at Portland as another Scorpion makes an initial approach overhead from the west, heading east. Note the mammoth wingtip pod containing the aircraft's rocket and missile armament. The ORANG flew the F-89H from 1957 until late 1960.

M.Sgt. Richard Rosenthal, weapons loading supervisor, loads 2.75-inch Folding-Fin Aerial Rockets (FFAR) into the wingtip pod of an F-89H. The Scorpion was the first ORANG combat aircraft not to have a gun armament, and the H-model carried 42 FFAR and also up to six Falcon air-to-air missiles, with half of each of these weapons in each large wingtip pod.

An ORANG F-89H fires a salvo of 2.75-inch rockets. Rockets with inert warheads were fired by aircrew in annual training ranges, both out over the ocean and inland, often at a Del Mar aerial target towed by another aircraft such as a T-33.

Operations are underway on the new ANG ramp at Portland in this aerial view from the late 1950s. Two T-33s and 21 F-89s are present. Note some variations in the black paint applied to the outside of the wingtip pods on the Scorpions. The new ANG hangar was dedicated in September 1956 and was built at a cost of $681,000.

Oregon Air Guardsmen take an ice cream break during summer training in this late-1950s picture. From left to right are an unidentified youth, M.Sgt. Roy McGinnis (electric shop supervisor), A2c. L. Luther, and A2c. C. Lockyear.

This view shows the 142nd Aircraft Control and Warning Flight (AC&W Flight) operations center after the Korean War. Note the radar display, an OA-99 search scope. The switch box on the right of the scope is for the GTA-6 communications center, used for the phone and radios. Men behind the vertical plotting board in the center manually reverse mark positions of air contacts for the operations staff in front.

The 142nd AC&W Flight conducted summer training at Pasa Robles Airport in California during 1956. Sitting on the FPS-4/TPS-10D height-finder is CWO3 Darl Jordan with an unidentified Air Guardsman. In the distance is the operations tent, and behind that is the TPS-1D search radar.

Capt. Wally Fellman is ready to fly as he stands atop an F-89H in this late 1950s picture. He was a veteran of the Korean War, where he flew 109 combat missions in F-86 Sabres with the 336th Fighter Squadron. He was credited with shooting down four enemy MiG-15 fighters between March and June 1953, as well as credit for one probable MiG destroyed and another one damaged.

Portland KPTV Channel 12 weather girl Geri Lindsey is surrounded by members of the 123rd Weather Flight during her base visit in February 1958. Flight members showed her the facsimile machine, Teletype, barograph, and other forecasting equipment. She later saw a weather briefing given to 123rd FIS aircrew. Flight commander Maj. Kenneth Githens (holding the pencil) shows Lindsey a chart; M.Sgt. Ronald Melcher is at extreme left, and all the others pictured are unidentified.

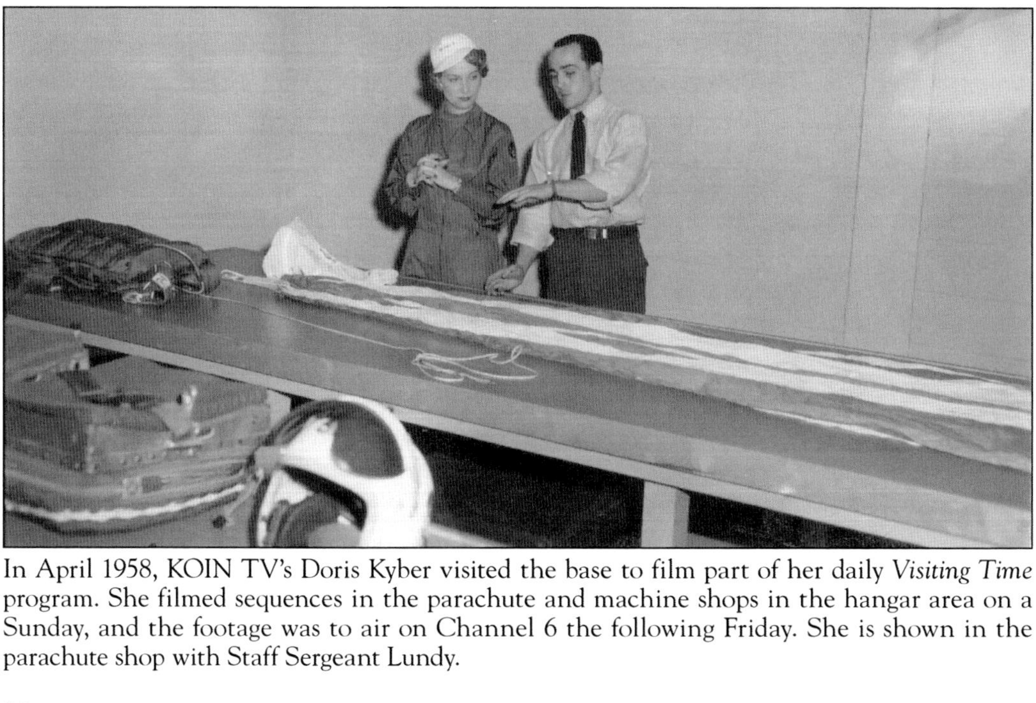

In April 1958, KOIN TV's Doris Kyber visited the base to film part of her daily *Visiting Time* program. She filmed sequences in the parachute and machine shops in the hangar area on a Sunday, and the footage was to air on Channel 6 the following Friday. She is shown in the parachute shop with Staff Sergeant Lundy.

The 142nd Supply Squadron ensured unit and personnel requirements were met, even at summer encampments where it seemed someone always forgot to bring something. At Gowen Field in 1957, A3c. Robert Noble of the 123rd FIS receives a pair of shoes from supply members, who are, from left to right, S.Sgt. Raymond Dragowsky, M.Sgt. Luther Leonard, and M.Sgt. Ivan Soelberg.

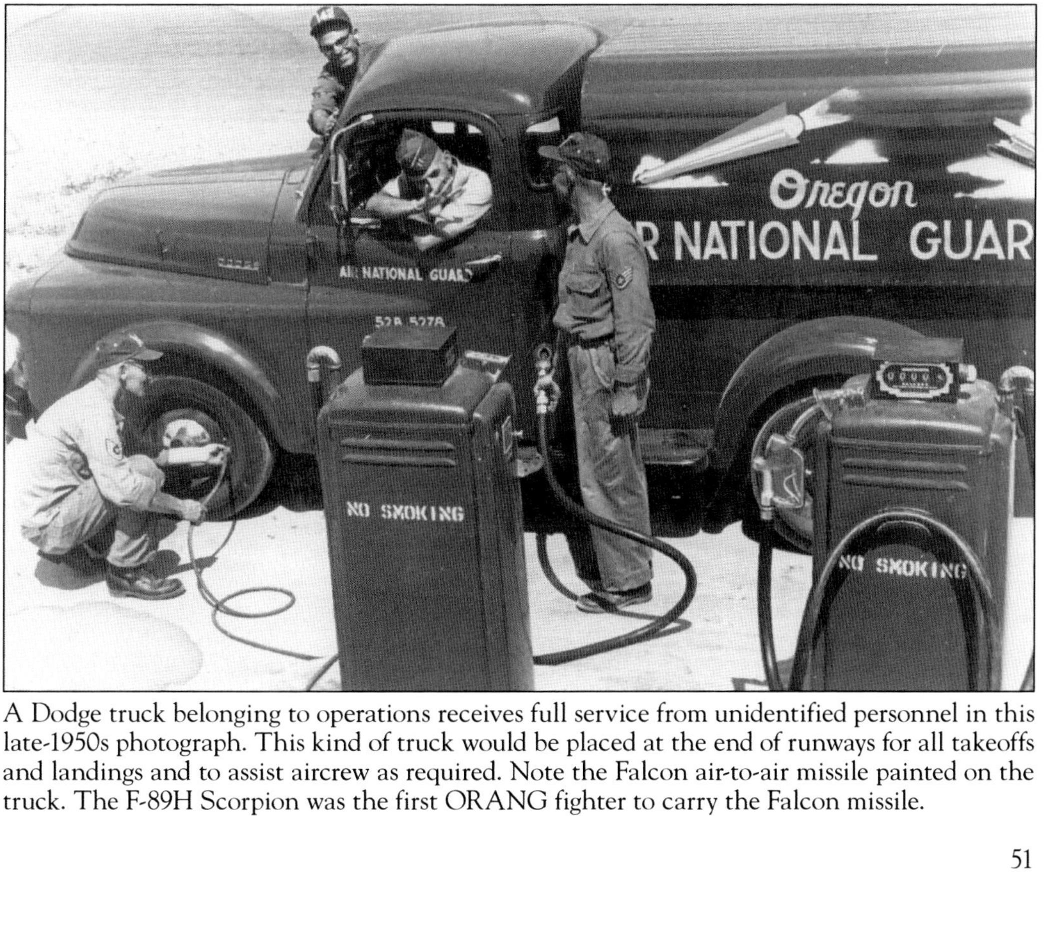

A Dodge truck belonging to operations receives full service from unidentified personnel in this late-1950s photograph. This kind of truck would be placed at the end of runways for all takeoffs and landings and to assist aircrew as required. Note the Falcon air-to-air missile painted on the truck. The F-89H Scorpion was the first ORANG fighter to carry the Falcon missile.

Members of the Oregon National Guard, including Maj. Gen. Thomas Rilea at the far right (sitting), watch F-86s above flown by the Colorado ANG Minute Men flight demonstration team while at summer training at Gowen Field, Idaho, in 1958. The Minute Men appear to be conducting a "corkscrew roll" maneuver, in which two wingmen make slow rolls around the lead and slot aircraft.

This ORANG T-33 with specially modified wingtip pods was flown in airborne nuclear sampling during the Operation Plumbbob series of nuclear tests in Nevada in 1957. The aircraft, aircrew, and maintainers had to be monitored for a while afterward to ensure there was no problem with radiation.

ORANG master sergeants stand in front of a 123rd FIS F-89H. They enlisted in 1946 and periodically reenlisted together. From left to right are ? Wilburn, Fred Boero, David Allen, George Schorder, Renny Jorgensen, Clarence McIntosh, Wilbur Eichelberg, Edward Pieka, Neil Buley, John Loins, Victor Struznik, Wally Bothum, Jack Cronise, Joe Holas, Ed Eichelberg, and Charles Bourcier, an original 123rd Observation Squadron member.

The ORANG's NCO Academy held its first class in 1958, Oregon's centennial year. In honor of the centennial, members were allowed to grow beards. From left to right are (first row) Clarence McIntosh, Charles Thompson Jr., Gene Thomas, and Richard Rosenthal; (second row) Jim Stewart, Bossom Mitchell, Wayne Kuhn, Bernard Verbout, Lewis Trujillo, and Jerry Leibert; (third row) Robert Betcher, Samuel Ierulli, Theodore George Jr., Robert Cain, Arthur Luft, David Price, and Leslie Thompson.

In this picture, Maj. David "Doc" Stoddard and Capt. Faith Hunsdon review paperwork. Captain Hunsdon became the first female member of the ORANG in March 1958 and served as a flight nurse in the 142nd Infirmary. She enlisted in the Air Force Reserve in 1951, gained her commission, and served on active duty before she joined the ORANG.

In the past, a lot more manual labor was required to prepare meals, and kitchen police (KP) duty was a routine temporary task for many junior enlisted Air Guardsmen. Here, an unidentified airman third class cuts potatoes.

An Oregon aircrew relaxes with hot cups of coffee during the 1960 summer camp held at Portland Air Base. From left to right are Phil Janney, unidentified (possibly Ken Solomon or Jerry Long), and Bill Kingery.

T.Sgt. Gene Thomas (left) instructs an unidentified airman second class on maintaining the nose gear assembly of an F-89. An F-89 would go through about 120 nose wheel tires every year (60 on each side), which averaged 31 landings per tire.

Forty-one aircrew from the 123rd FIS gather for a squadron picture on a sunny afternoon by an F-89H on the ramp outside the ORANG hangar in this late-1950s view.

The *Richfield Success Story* television program profiled successful businesses and activities with a connection to Richfield oil products and covered the ORANG through KGW-TV Channel 8 in one of its locally sponsored shows in June 1960. Above, from left to right, are program announcer Bill Nielson, maintenance officer Capt. William Harlow, and an unidentified cameraman. They view a portion of an Allison J-35 turbojet engine from an F-89H Scorpion fighter.

A large formation of ORANG F-89Hs passes overhead during the ending ceremony for annual summer training at Portland on June 25, 1960. It was near the end of the F-89H's service and was, according the June 1960 issue of *Air Scoop*, a "maximum effort" led by Col. Patrick O'Grady. The small covers over the rocket ports in the wingtip pods were removed, creating a non-jet sound reportedly more like that of a formation of propeller-driven B-17 bombers.

A Del Mar aerial towed target is shown under the left wing of an ORANG T-33 in October 1960. The brightly painted target was let out with a cable well behind the tow aircraft for the F-89 fighters to attack. The small pod to the right is for generating cable reel electrical power. Depending on the type of mission and outcome, it could be reeled in again for use at another time.

ORANG Air Guardsmen welcome the arrival of the first F-89J to Portland in August 1960. This example of the ultimate F-89J variant came from the South Dakota ANG. Essentially a converted F-89D, the F-89J featured an improved fire control system. Its wingtip pod weapons were replaced with fuel tanks and weapons pylons were added under the wing to carry air-to-air missiles or the large MB-1 rocket.

Citizen airmen of the ORANG have long been involved in charity and volunteer work in the local community in a variety of ways. Seen here are unidentified Air and Army Guard NCOs lifting a Portland Police Sunshine Division barrel during the food and Toy N Joy Makers drives that took place several days before Christmas in 1960.

Three

1960s

Earning the Spurs

In July 1961, the 123rd Fighter Interceptor Squadron, or FIS, first began 24-hour alert operations as the Air National Guard took on a greater role in US Air Force's Air Defense Command operations. This took place as the Cold War threat grew more complex with Soviet development of the intercontinental ballistic missile in addition to its evolving nuclear bomber threat.

Due to the F-89J's departure from active-duty service following the arrival of newer Century Series fighters in May 1962, the ORANG took on a schoolhouse-like role, training F-89 radar intercept officers for the eight ANG units that comprised the remaining F-89 community. Reflecting this significant responsibility, mission accomplishment, and the unit's overall efficiency, in January 1963, the 123rd FIS received the Air Force Outstanding Unit award, an ANG first.

A humanitarian role for the ORANG also emerged. In June 1960, the ORANG's C-47 returned four Oregon polio patients home from California. In another helpful operation, though not humanitarian per se, on April 18, 1964, a 123rd FIS F-89 aircrew demonstrated superior all-weather airmanship when they successfully located and assisted a lost civilian propeller-driven plane in some formidable weather over California.

By early 1966, with the Vietnam War escalating and active-duty air defense forces being cut back, the ORANG made another aircraft transition. The F-89 was replaced by the single-seat Convair F-102A Delta Dagger. This left the 123rd FIS solely accountable for all air defense alert responsibilities executed from Portland Air Base.

This passed-along air defense responsibility was a prelude of the future. In July 1968, the USAF turned responsibility for administration of Portland Air Base over to the ORANG.

Another sign of the future occurred in January 1969, when Linda Schoonmaker became the ORANG's first female non–prior service enlistee. This demonstrated increased awareness of opportunities for citizens to serve in the ANG directly without first serving on active duty.

A 123rd FIS aircrew saddles into an F-89J in October 1961. Pilot Brad Newell is in the front seat, and George Smith is on the ladder. The two-seat F-89 held a pilot to fly the aircraft and a radar intercept officer to operate the relatively sophisticated Hughes fire control systems of that time.

This view shows the maintenance control center, also known as "the Bubble." It was built by M.Sgt. Lloyd Buckley and first used in the summer of 1960. S.Sgt. Eugene Jaramello (left) and Staff Sergeant Mitchell control flight line maintenance. The view was superb. It had a unique status board on the center console and a 12-channel intercom to communicate with a variety of shops to expedite timely maintenance actions.

In June 1961, the ORANG held its annual field training at Portland Air Base. Here, a group of Air Guardsmen from the 142nd Consolidated Aircraft Maintenance Squadron (CAMS) hold a polishing party during this summer training to bring the natural metal finish of an F-89J to full luster, perhaps in preparation for a VIP visit.

CWO4 Bud Wilson and C.M.Sgt. Richard Rosenthal go over a training version of the MB-1 (later designated AIR-2A) Genie unguided air-to-air rocket at Portland in January 1961. Weighing more than 800 pounds and stretching over nine feet in length, the Genie was the most powerful air-to-air weapon available for USAF interceptors of the day and could be carried by the ORANG's F-89Js and F-101Bs.

The ORANG established a 32-piece drum and bugle corps in mid-1960 that frequently participated in base, military, and community events such as the Merrykana and Rose Festival parades. Here the corps marches past the Memorial Coliseum in the early 1960s

The ORANG Precision Rifle Team, followed by the drum and bugle corps, marches down SW Fifth Avenue during the May 1962 Armed Forces Day Parade in Portland. The 26-member team's origins dated to December 1960. It served as an ORANG honor guard and competitive drill team, taking part in many community parades and often in company with the drum and bugle corps.

In 1964, the ORANG's 244th Radio Relay Squadron deployed for summer training to Hog Ranch Ridge in Yakima, Washington. A pair of trucks is seen here, operationally configured at this remote site. The one on the right holds the FM radio relay antennas, oriented in two directions to connect with two other relay sites. This site could transmit or receive a message, amplify it, and retransmit to the next relay point.

An array of equipment occupies acreage near the Redmond, Oregon, airport during ANG summer training in August 1965. The long row of vans in the foreground includes the 142nd Mobile Communications Squadron's torn-tape Teletype relay center (based in an expanded van) and FM radio shelters on trucks of the 221st and 244th Radio Relay Squadrons. Above the row of vans and in the center of the picture are four pairs of radio-transmit shelters.

The ORANG took on responsibility for training the F-89J radar intercept officers of eight ANG squadrons in October 1962. Active-duty instructors assisted in the classroom at Portland while the ORANG provided F-89s for use by each class of students in the 15-week course. Facing the audience at a class graduation are, from left to right, Capt. William Hearn, Brig. Gen. Gordon Doolittle, Lt. Col. Robert Stacklie, and Maj. James Thomas.

An ORANG flight line maintenance flight stands by its F-89J on the Portland ramp in this March 1964 picture, probably taken over a drill weekend when all flight members, including the part-time traditional Air Guardsmen, were present for training. From left to right are (first row) M.Sgt. Reub Vermilyea, S.Sgt. Denny Cox, and flight chief M.Sgt. Bob Edgerton; (second row) A1c. Ron Edwards and S.Sgt. Ben Jacks. (Courtesy of Ron Edwards.)

In August 1964, the ORANG fielded a team to compete in the Ricks Trophy competition held at Tyndall Air Force Base in Florida. From left to right are (first row) Bill Harlow, Jim Wingo, Labe Walton, Brad Newell, Raymond Kincaid, William Kingery, Gary Markstaller, and Marvin Brandt; (second row) Bill McAuley, Ed Bauder, Art Clulow, Gene Thomas, unidentified, Dick Chambers, Paul Chapmen, Richard Rosenthal, Ken McCoy, Dick Bay, and Edwin Eichelberg.

Pilot Rick Friberg and an unidentified officer conduct their preflight checks on an F-89J that has just been brought into the alert barn at Portland. The F-89 was the first interceptor for which a dedicated alert facility was constructed at Portland. After a jet was brought there, aircrew checked it and ensured switches and controls were set, ready to enable a speedy departure in case of a scramble order.

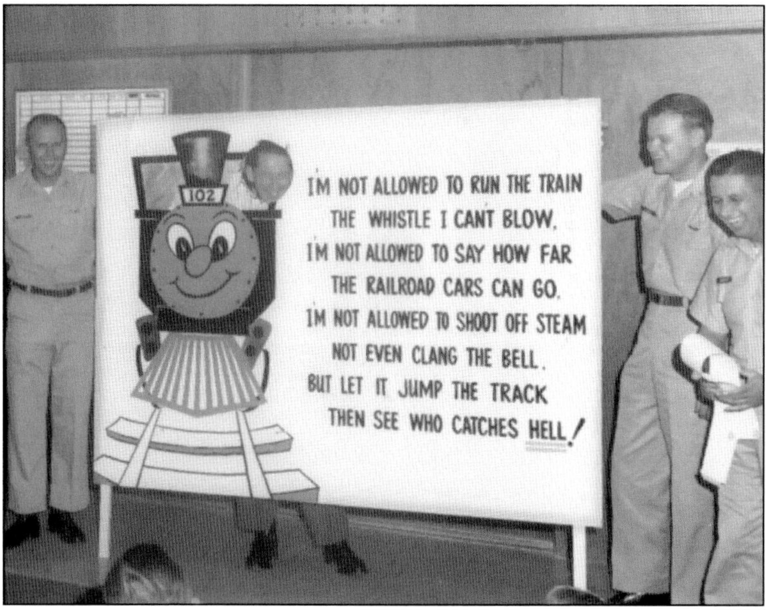

A 123rd FIS aircrew shares a hearty laugh in the squadron's aircrew briefing room in Portland in the 1960s. From left to right are Gene White, 123rd FIS commander Raymond Kincaid, ? Busse, and Joseph Judge.

Members of the publications distribution office (PDO) are ready for business. The PDO was the focal point for the unit receipt of official publications, regulations, technical orders, and such, and from the PDO, these publications, changes, and updates would be distributed to the various units and organizations. From left to right are an unidentified airman first class, A1c. Wayne Pierce, S.Sgt. Everett Brown (standing), and T.Sgt. Bryce Barrett (sitting with cigar).

In this c. 1964 picture, Air Guardsman A3c. Fred Jennings looks at transmit bank equipment in the 142nd Mobile Communications Squadron's torn-tape Teletype relay center van.

In 1965, the Defense Department announced air defense cuts, and the active-duty unit at Portland Air Base was on the list. On January 5, 1966, the 337th Fighter Group's 460th FIS turned over the first of 20 F-102 fighters to the 142nd FG in a ceremony. Here, 337th FG commander Col. Charles Praul reviews the aircraft forms binder with 142nd FG commander Col. Patrick O'Grady.

A crew chief with the 142nd CAMS, M.Sgt. Raymond Dahm, helps 123rd FIS pilot Capt. Brian Freeman strap into an F-102. Note the shamrock abaft the canopy glazing, indicating that this was the aircraft of 142nd FG commander Col. Patrick O'Grady.

In this 1960s view, an Oregon F-102 thunders off the runway in afterburner and into the weather at Portland.

The front of the 142nd FG's 1966 Christmas card was the first to reflect the ORANG's new F-102 Delta Dart fighter interceptor.

A c. 1966 aerial view of the ORANG facilities at Portland Air Base shows F-102s and T-33s on the ramp with F-102s occupying the alert barns to the upper left of the Guard ramp. Note the air rescue HU-16 Albatross seaplanes on the AF Reserve ramp in the upper left and the lone F-89 on static display at the bottom right.

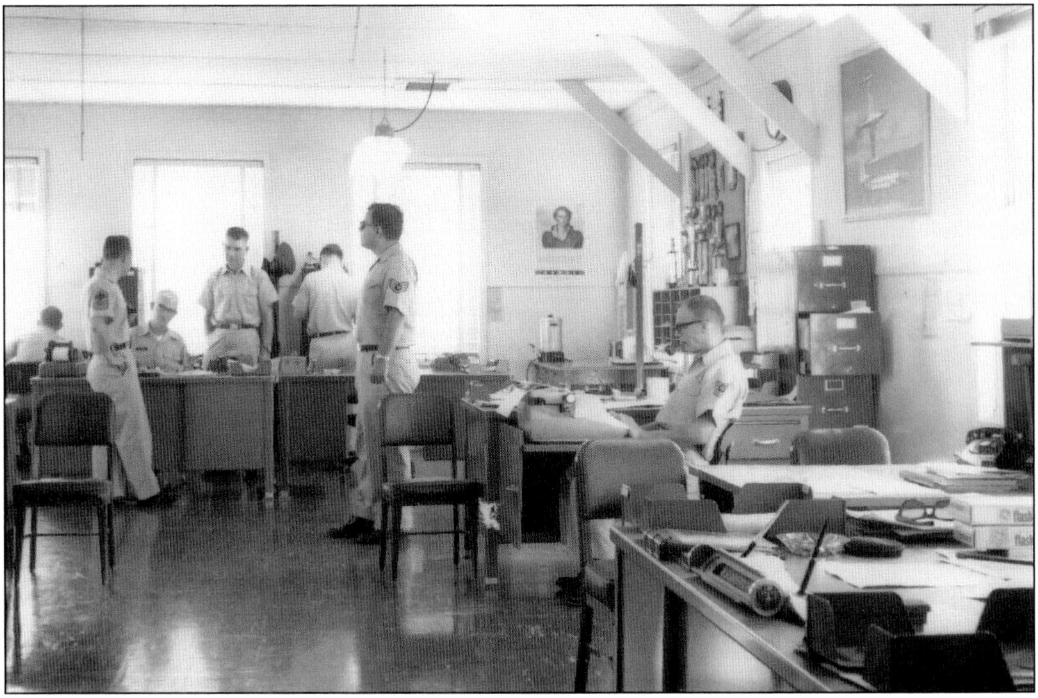

This c. 1968 view shows the 142nd FG headquarters administrative office area. From left to right are unidentified, S.M.Sgt. Wilfred Unverricht, M.Sgt. Marion Wilbourn, Maj. David Pahlka, an unidentified staff sergeant, S.Sgt. Richard Calidion, and T.Sgt. ? Keller.

Deployed vehicles of the 244th Mobile Communications Squadron are operationally arrayed in this mid- to late-1960s view, possibly taken near a state armory building, which is behind the vehicles to the right of the flagpole. One FM radio relay antenna is operationally configured atop the truck at the left.

ANG crew chiefs are notorious for their pride in caring for their assigned aircraft. T.Sgt. Ron Edwards did his best with his Convair F-102A-80-CO Delta Dagger 56-1466, but it refused to cooperate with paint, as seen here in January 1969. It shed paint despite his care, perhaps evidence of a prior issue with fuel or hydraulic fluids. He told others his "Deuce" (a nickname for the F-102) "flew so fast, the paint wouldn't stay on." (Courtesy of Ron Edwards.)

In this late 1960s photograph, a crew chief signals an ORANG F-102 to approach straight along a wet taxiway at Portland International. This is probably an end-of-runway, last-chance check prior to takeoff.

Weapons loaders use a loading frame to emplace an AIM-4 Falcon air-to-air missile into the missile bay of an Oregon F-102. The F-102 could carry up to six of these AIM-4 missiles internally. Of the four men, only Joe Woodburn, third from the left with a visible face, is identified.

T.Sgt. Billy Magar services a 123rd FIS TF-102A with liquid oxygen (LOX) before a flight. The TF-102A, affectionately called the "Tub," was the training version of the F-102 Delta Dagger and featured side-by-side seating. Note the open missile bay containing AIM-4 Falcon Weapon System Evaluator Missiles (WSEM) forward and aft in the portside missile bay. Enclosing the armament helped maximize performance of the F-102.

Pilot Brian Freeman conducts a preflight inspection of an Oregon F-102 on the Portland ramp before a sortie.

Lt. Col. Albert Garvin, commander of the 142nd Mobile Communications Squadron from March 1968 to September 1969, smiles as he holds the award presented to his squadron for being the ORANG's Outstanding Unit of 1968.

A young ORANG F-102 pilot, Lieutenant Busse, pauses for a photograph atop his steed.

In 1966, the ORANG traded in its C-47 support aircraft for a Douglas VC-54E Skymaster, reportedly the former aircraft of the 25th Air Division commander. Here, an Oregon F-102 tries to stay in formation long enough for a picture with the C-54 near Mount Hood. The jet pilot increased his angle of attack in an effort to slow down long enough for the camera to capture the scene.

In this late 1960s picture, an Oregon Air Guard F-102 four-ship formation plies the skies above the Columbia River. The tail pipe of the nearest jet is just above Multnomah Falls, with the Bonneville Dam in the distance to the east at the top of the picture.

Oregon Air Guardsmen work to repair vandal damage to an F-89H on outdoor display at the Oregon Museum of Science and Industry (OMSI) in Washington Park in Portland, Oregon, in 1968. The former ORANG aircraft was donated to OMSI in 1961 after the 123rd FIS converted to the F-89J.

U.S. AIR FORCE
AIR GUARD
142d
CAM SQ.

Members of the 142nd CAMS gathered for a picture around 1968 with a brace of the Convair F-102 Delta Daggers they were responsible for maintaining between 1966 and 1971. (Courtesy of Gene Thomas.)

Oregon Air Guardsmen from either the 142nd and/or the 244th Mobile Communications Squadron fire the M1 carbine during small arms training at Camp Bonneville in Washington around 1969. In this time frame, these squadrons performed their weekend drill duty on a different weekend from the 142nd FG, given the limited parking and food service spaces on Portland Air Base when all units were present.

On January 11, 1969, Brig. Gen. Staryl Austin (left) enlisted Linda Schoonmaker as the first non–prior service female enlistee in the ORANG. She was one of several Schoonmakers to proudly serve with the ORANG through its history.

In 1969, the ORANG's "Doolittle Raiders" went to Ellington Field, Texas, to study how the 147th FG won an Air Force Outstanding Unit award. From left to right are (first row) Zane Harper, Bob Renn, Ivar Anderson, David Pahlka, Herb Riley, and Bud Opitz; (second row) ? Higgenlacher, Eugene Bouton, Denny Madison, Gene Thomas, Vernon Quick, unidentified, Bob Cain, and John Miller; (third row) two unidentified men, Tom Eder, Edward Hoeksre, unidentified, Ed Pahlka, Airman Ramsey, and two unidentified men.

F-102s approach an M42 Duster self-propelled anti-aircraft gun during National Guard field training in the 1960s. The ORANG provided aerial harassment during summer training when requested by Oregon's Army National Guard, which had the M42 Duster in its inventory during the Cold War years.

In 1970, the 142nd FG received the Aerospace Defense Command "A" Award for outstanding achievement during the period from July 1968 through August 1969. The award recognized performance that led to higher standards of sustained operational effectiveness. At the award ceremony in Portland, from left to right, are Col. Patrick O'Grady (holding the award flag), Maj. Gen. Archie Burke (commander, 25th Air Division), and an unidentified colonel.

Shown here in 1970 are the ORANG pilots who flew at the William Tell Air-to-Air Weapons meet at Tyndall Air Force Base in Florida when the unit placed second in the F-102 category. The ORANG soon built upon the lessons learned from this experience. From left to right are (front row) Michael Ranslam and Harold Hoffman; (second row) Patrick O'Grady, Bill McDonald, Jim Angel, and Bob Parker.

Four

1970s
Medicine Men and Women

As the decade began, America's role in Vietnam was decreasing. However, the ORANG expanded to its largest ever manpower authorization with the formation of five tactical air control units that provided air surveillance and battle management functions. In part, this reflected the development of the post-draft Total Force concept, in which the ANG assumed a more deliberately planned role in the nation's defense.

As the ORANG added additional units, it also established other operating locations. In 1971, the 104th Tactical Control Squadron (TCS) began operations at Kingsley Field near Klamath Falls, Oregon.

The ORANG also expanded ties to the community with the development and inauguration of the Housing Authority of Portland (HAP) Camp. Known as Camp Rosenbaum today, it is an annual summer camp for disadvantaged youth held at Camp Rilea on the Oregon coast.

Early in the decade, the ORANG converted to the two-seat McDonnell F-101B Voodoo fighter interceptor. With the F-101, the ORANG distinguished itself in the air defense community.

Humanitarian support requests from the community continued to be serviced. In August 1972, a 123rd FIS crew flew a jet-speed mercy mission in an F-101 to help save an infant in Boise, Idaho. More were to follow.

As an example of the ORANG's readiness and capability, in 1976, the 142nd Fighter Interceptor Group (FIG) won top honors at a pair of Aerospace Defense Command (ADC) competitions, the Weapons Loading Competition and the famous William Tell Air-to-Air Weapons Meet, in which a 123rd FIS aircrew garnered the contest's overall Top Gun award.

As the Air Force put Vietnam War lessons learned into practice in the Flag series exercise program, the ORANG also took part in these integrated airpower exercises to boost its combat skills. For example, the ORANG's 104th TCS was the first Forward Air Control Party to participate in a Red Flag exercise in 1977.

In addition to sharpening skills in combined elements of airpower, the ORANG grew more into joint operations with other branches of the service. In 1979, the 123rd Weather Flight's mission changed to providing meteorological support for the Oregon Army National Guard's 41st Infantry Brigade.

This aerial view of the ORANG ramp in Portland was captured after the arrival of the F-101. The alert facility introduced in the F-89 era is at bottom right, from which interceptors were scrambled. Behind the alert barn, an F-101 rests with its front end covered by a portable nose dock, a flight line shelter helpful in protection from the rain of the Pacific Northwest. Note the static display F-89 and F-102 near the top of the picture.

F-101 aircrew of the 123rd FIS relax before their briefing in the squadron's main briefing room during a 1972 readiness exercise. In the foreground, from left to right, are George Cathey, Bill McDonald, and Mike Fisher. In the background, from left to right, are Jack Loacker, G.W. Sorenson, Everett Bernhardt, and an unidentified aircrew member.

This c. February 1973 view shows an ORANG F-101B being readied in the Portland alert barn. Weapons loaders prepare to load an AIM-4 Falcon air-to-air missile on the aircraft. One AIM-4 is already loaded on the aircraft. A pilot's helmet is on the canopy rail, and an electrical power cable and pneumatic line are attached to help quickly start the aircraft in case of a scramble order.

An ORANG F-101F, more fully described as a McDonnell F-101F-106-MC Voodoo, takes to the skies in afterburner at Portland in this early 1970s photograph. The 79 F-101Fs produced were externally identical to the 479 F-101B interceptors but had dual flight controls for use as an operational/conversion trainer. They were fully combat capable, with the same armament as the F-101B. A few F models were found in each F-101B squadron.

Launch preparations for a pair of F-101s are underway at dusk in this early-1970s view of the Portland ANG ramp.

An ORANG F-101B properly configured for landing settles in as the speed brakes extend in this early-1970s photograph. The F-101 also had a drag parachute to help it decelerate once it landed and rolled out down the runway.

The ORANG Cessna U-3B rests on the Portland ramp in July 1972. Popularly known as the "Blue Canoe," it was a military version of the Cessna 310F and was used for light administrative liaison, cargo, and utility tasks.

An unidentified operations NCO wearing the diamond of a first sergeant updates the flying schedule board at the 123rd FIS duty desk some time in 1971 or 1972, in the early days after the ORANG received the F-101.

When forest fires threatened the city of Klamath Falls, Oregon, in August 1973, Oregon Air Guardsmen from the 104th Tactical Control Squadron helped with fighting the fires, assisted with evacuations, and operated a field kitchen. The ORANG has provided a variety of services and capabilities in combating forest fires, including the efforts described here and more, such as providing communications in remote areas to aid in firefighting coordination.

In July 1973, base civil engineer chief Col. Benjamin Hawkins retired after a 37-year career with a full-scale retirement ceremony including a pass in review at Portland Air Base. In the jeep from left to right are Brig. Gen Patrick O'Grady. (ORANG deputy chief of staff), Maj. Gen. Richard Miller (the adjutant general of Oregon), C.M.Sgt. Pete Trotogott (the first chief master sergeant of the ORANG, driving), and Colonel Hawkins.

Lt. Col. William McDonald reviews paperwork in the aircraft forms binder at planeside in the Portland alert facility. Flying and maintenance forms such as the AFTO (Air Force Technical Order) 781 series of checklists are used to document mission and aircrew data and record any mechanical discrepancies on a given aircraft.

Camp Bonneville in Washington State, an Army installation active from 1910 until defense cuts forced it to close in 1995, was frequently used by the ORANG for nonflying training tasks that could be completed over a weekend of Air Guard drill training, such as a unit's annual small-arms qualification firing. This view shows vehicles of the 142nd Mobile Communications Squadron at Camp Bonneville before the unit's inactivation in June 1971.

Roger Hawkins (back to camera) and an unidentified Air Guardsman unload an AIM-4 WSEM from an F-101. The WSEMs were training devices that interacted with the aircraft's systems to simulate a live missile. The unloading action appears to be happening in between flights, as the single-point refueling access door is open and the cap is off and dangling by the chain.

Members of the Consolidated Aircraft Maintenance Squadron (CAMS) parachute shop pause for this photograph in the 1970s. They ensured that aircrew parachutes and drag parachutes were packed and maintained to function properly for the unit's aircrew F-101 aircraft. From left to right are T.Sgt. Larry Holas, M.Sgt. Ed Hager (supervisor), Lois Oster (rank obscured), Sr.A. Lee Jansen, and S.Sgt. Gary McKinzie.

In this 1970s view, the Portland Air Base Fire Department conducts an aircrew extraction drill at an F-101. This core base fire department task requires proficiency and is usually evaluated by inspectors during local operational readiness exercises and higher headquarters inspections.

A trio of ORANG F-101s rumbles west from the Portland ramp as their J57 engines kick up accumulated dust. The trio is probably en route to the approach end of runway 10R for a takeoff. Three is an irregular number for a tactical formation, but if no aerial targets were available for two-ship intercept training, such as a T-33, a trio of fighters could be launched for air intercept training with target duties rotated between them.

The 116th Tactical Control Squadron operations center is shown in this image captured inside an S-80 shelter in the mid-1970s. The illuminated plotting board in the front stretched across the width of the S-80 and showed the radar-derived plot of air contact information and other operational data that enabled the squadron to fulfill its responsibility within the ground theater air control system.

Sr.A. Kiamichi Isham of the 116th TCS (Control and Reporting Center) looks up from her position at a UPA-35 Search Radar Indicator in the 1970s. Information displayed on the UPA-35 provided azimuth, range, and height data for a target detected by search and height-finding radars, which permitted control and direction of military aircraft from the 116th operations center.

At Portland's open house in 1975, the ORANG adopted an F-14 Tomcat of Navy squadron VX-4. Shown here is the F-14 wearing the Keith Ferris camouflage scheme, which was used temporarily in the 1970s, and bearing the ANG emblem and Oregon state identifier. The Keith Ferris camouflage was a deceptive paint scheme consisting of three shades of gray applied in a serrated pattern.

In June 1976, the ORANG fielded a float to participate in the Bicentennial Starlight Parade in Portland's Rose Festival. The float's patriotic theme included personnel in uniforms depicting the militia of 1776, complete with a Liberty Bell replica, and the Oregon Air Guard of 1976, featuring a trio of scale model F-101s.

On October 25, 1976, President Ford briefly visited Portland, Oregon. He took time to congratulate the ORANG's champions of Aerospace Defense Command's worldwide weapons loading championship of May 1976. Facing the president, from left to right, are T.Sgt. Lane Hoffman, T.Sgt. Joe Woodburn, T.Sgt. Mark Wiebold, and S.M.Sgt. Alan Kaser. They won with two near-perfect loads, a high test score, and maximum points on the tools and equipment check.

M.Sgt. Armand Labelle epitomized the dedicated professionalism and hard work of the ground crews to maintain their aircraft in a mission-ready status. Here, he cleans the windshield of an F-101 at the William Tell 1978 air defense meet. He earned his enlisted aircrew wings as a flying crew chief with the ORANG's C-45, C-47, C-54, and C-131 transport aircraft and accrued some 2,200 flight hours.

In the famous biennial William Tell air defense meet held at Tyndall Air Force Base in Florida during late 1976, the 142nd FIG garnered first place in the F-101 category. Shown here before the competition, S.Sgt. Curtis Scott presents an apple and arrow representing the contest to one of the ORANG aircrew that participated, Maj. Brad Newell (left) and Lt. Col. Don Tonole. This aircrew earned the meet's overall Top Gun title.

One of the ORANG F-101s that competed in the 1976 William Tell air defense competition rests on the ramp during the meet, held in October and November. Parked to the right are F-106s of the 87th FIS from K.I. Sawyer Air Force Base in Michigan. (Courtesy of Marty Isham.)

This picture was taken of the ORANG's winning team at the 1976 William Tell meet, in which the 142nd FIG won the F-101 category. Of note in the second row, the second person in from the right is Canadian Forces control technician Cpl. Al Currie, from the 25th Air Division, who was part of the team. Also present is the author's 1970s neighbor John Gallant, third from the right in the back row.

The legendary general Daniel "Chappie" James Jr. (right), commander of the North American Aerospace Defense Command and the USAF Aerospace Defense Command, presents the William Tell 1976 winning team, F-101 category, trophy to the ORANG's team leader, Lt. Col. Marty Bergan, commander of the 123rd FIS. The engaging woman assisting in between them is identified only as "Miss Interceptor."

An Oregon F-101B soars over downtown Portland, Oregon, above the landmark Fremont Bridge spanning the Willamette River. The two-digit call sign number painted aft on the speed brake was something the ORANG began using in the mid-1970s; it was such a handy reference number for operations, maintenance, and even civilian air traffic controllers that the numbers were continued in service through the rest of the F-101 era.

A pair of F-101Bs flies near a snow- and cloud-covered mountain, possibly Mount Hood, in the late 1970s. For operations during the frequently rainy Pacific Northwest winter, Oregon F-101s often carried an external fuel tank in order to have sufficient fuel in case the weather at home base deteriorated and forced a divert to an alternate airfield for recovery.

The Oregon Convair C-131 Samaritan replaced the C-54 support aircraft in 1972. Here, it flies above a snow-covered forest with an F-101 escort, possibly the same aircraft in the previous image, in the late 1970s. (Courtesy of Marty Isham.)

In October 1977, ORANG maintainers held an F-101 egress certification class at the jet. Among the men assembled here are Chuck Marshall, Charlie Bourcier, Chuck Estes, Paul Miller, Armand Labelle, Ron Hottenroth, Joe Holas, Mike Ryan, Ray Dahm, Ralph Grandy, Vern Marshall, Elvis Tracy, Clarence MacIntosh, and Carl Boudeau. The class was an annual training requirement.

Making the most effective and efficient use of the ANG hangar in Portland is a bit like choreographing a ballet. Aircraft are moved in and out for maintenance and regular hangar cleaning, so aircraft are constantly re-spotted (or repositioned). Pictured in the late 1970s, an F-101, minus ejection seats, canopy, and assorted panels, is backed out of the hangar during a re-spot while it is not raining.

Air Guardsmen service an Oregon T-33 in this view of the Portland ramp from the 1970s. An unidentified NCO fills the left wingtip tank while a man who is possibly S.M.Sgt. Art Dierickx fills the right wing tank. Being of an older design, the T-33 did not have the single-point refueling capability of later aircraft, but it was a well-regarded and reliable aircraft.

Maj. Gen. Gordon Doolittle retired from the ORANG in June 1977. He was a World War II combat veteran who joined the Oregon Guard in 1946. He served at various levels of command in the ORANG and at the National Guard Bureau, strongly influencing both. Here, a flight of F-101s roars overhead. The men are, from left to right, unidentified, Brig. Gen. Patrick O'Grady, and Major General Doolittle.

The 123rd Weather Flight's personnel work to prepare vugraph overhead projector slides for a weather update briefing. From left to right are advisor Rod Gaudreau, Steve Hansen, and Robin Brooks.

Ready to fly in an F-101 at Portland in this 1970s view are Maj. Bob Parker (left), 123rd FIS, and Maj. Gen. Richard Miller, the Oregon adjutant general. Note the small windscreen behind the pilot, designed to provide the back-seated passenger with some cover from the slipstream in case of inadvertent canopy loss.

Aviation-minded citizens roam the ANG ramp at Portland, viewing a variety of ANG, Air Force Reserve, Air Force, Navy, and Marine Corps aircraft during an open house in the late 1970s. The air defense alert facility is seen at the top of the image with four places for alert aircraft, ready to scramble. The crew area from which aircrew ran to their planes was located between the first and second shelter.

An F-101B with a Redhawk on the tail soars in the sun in this late-1970s view. The Redhawk clutches a banner in his talons bearing the symbol for the USAF Outstanding Unit award, with an oak leaf cluster to indicate multiple awards, as well as the state identification. The tiny "A" is the Aerospace Defense Command's award to units for sustained operational effectiveness, an ORANG trademark throughout its history.

The ORANG celebrated Pacific Northwest aviation at the 50th anniversary of Oregon's Hillsboro Airport in June 1978. A medical emergency sidelined the Thunderbirds, but five Oregon F-101s performed for the crowd of 60,000. It was one of the early reappearances of the Redhawk emblem on ORANG aircraft after a long absence. Shown are four F-101s, whilst the solo aircraft, out of sight in this image, set up for a swift flight down the field in the opposite direction, a move that caught the crowd by surprise.

Adult and youth at the HAP Camp, held at Camp Rilea near the Oregon coast in August 1978, enjoy the summer weather. Started in 1970 by an officer who later became ORANG leader, Brig. Gen. Fred Rosenbaum, this annual community service program for underprivileged youth is held at the same location and is now called Camp Rosenbaum. It's known as the Oregon Air Guard's largest community service project.

Comedian Bob Hope, well regarded by military personnel for his work with the armed forces and the USO, came through Portland Air Base during a visit to Oregon in July 1980. Here, he poses briefly with his golf club stage prop in front of the ORANG's welcome sign adjacent to the ANG ramp.

The arrival of the first McDonnell Douglas F-4C Phantom IIs in Portland on September 25, 1980, heralded the end of the F-101 era. The F-4s came from an Illinois ANG unit with a tactical fighter air-to-ground role. Oregon maintainers had a bit of work ahead of them to fine tune and optimize the performance of various components such as the air intercept radar for the strategic air defense mission.

Five

1980s

Phantom Pheats

The first McDonnell Douglas F-4 Phantom II fighters arrived in Portland in late 1980. With the Phantom, ORANG mission requirements increased, but Oregon's Air Guardians proved to be up for the challenge.

As active-duty fighter interceptor squadrons underwent further drawdown, more of the air defense mission went to the ANG. In July 1981, the 142nd FIG established Operating Location Alert Detachment (OLAD) at Kingsley Field in Oregon.

The ORANG soon made greater use of Kingsley. In January 1983, it established the 8123rd Fighter Interceptor Training Squadron and the strategic air defense schoolhouse at Kingsley Field. On April 1, 1983, the base was transferred from the USAF to the ORANG.

In 1984, the ORANG achieved success with the Phantom in the William Tell meet when the unit placed first in the F-4 category, flying and beating many of its F-15 Eagle and F-106 Delta Dart rivals in the competition. An ORANG aircrew won the overall F-4 Top Gun award.

The Cold War called from overseas in 1986, and Oregon Air Guardsmen participated in the yearlong Creek Klaxon air defense alert operation at Ramstein Air Base in West Germany. Aircrew and maintainers rotated to Germany to fly and fix ANG F-4D aircraft on Zulu Alert while Ramstein converted from the F-4 to the F-16.

Showing prowess in the Phantom, the ORANG again achieved distinction at the William Tell meet in 1986 when the 142nd FIG won F-4 Top Gun and Best Looking Aircraft, as well as the Arrival Timing and Special Achievement awards. More William Tell success followed in 1988, the last year for the F-4 to participate in the meet.

Change was constant in the 1980s. In March 1988, Kingsley Field began transition to the General Dynamics F-16 Fighting Falcon Air Defense Fighter (ADF) as the ANG's strategic air defense community transitioned from the F-4 to F-16. In October 1988, the 116th Tactical Control Squadron relocated from Portland to Camp Rilea in Warrenton, Oregon. Last but not least, in October 1989, the 142nd FIG completed its transition from the F-4 to the McDonnell Douglas F-15A Eagle.

Military-friendly air installations have a cable barrier at the ends of the runway in order to catch jets that may experience mechanical difficulty on takeoff or landing. Here, ORANG F-4C 776, still in South-East Asia livery, takes the barrier with tailhook down and drag chute deployed at Portland in 1982. Crew chief Doug Riese named her "Miss Piggy," and today, she resides in the Boeing Museum of Flight in Seattle.

When active-duty interceptor units withdrew from Kingsley Field in Klamath Falls, Oregon, in 1981, the ORANG filled the vacuum with OLAD, sending Portland F-4s and rotating aircrew to stand alert at Kingsley in addition to the alert operation in Portland. Here, Crew chief Bob Dean approaches a just-arrived F-4C with a crew ladder at the Kingsley alert facility.

ORANG aircrew enjoy a unique view of the scenic vistas in the Pacific Northwest. This Portland F-4C aircrew beholds such a scene as it passes near Mount Hood, with snowy peaks at Mount Saint Helens (left) and Mount Adams visible in the distance.

In July 1983, the 116th Tactical Control Squadron underwent an operational readiness inspection at Camp Rilea. Here, the squadron's TPS-43 radar is operationally configured, and underneath the camouflage net are the radar van, heat exchanger, and air conditioners. The operations center was located separately some distance away from the radar. The unidentified, smiling NCOs in the foreground are likely inspectors or observers.

In January 1983, the 8123rd Fighter Interceptor Training Squadron (later redesignated as the 114th Tactical Fighter Training Squadron) began operations at Kingsley Field. Here, Maj. Frank Romaglia (left) congratulates student 2nd Lt. Chris Sakamoto after the unit's first training sortie in February 1983. The 8123rd was the air defense schoolhouse for training the aircrew of the reserve component squadrons that flew the F-4C/D in the strategic air defense mission in the Cold War.

A Kingsley F-4C 114th Tactical Fighter Training Squadron (TFTS) makes its final approach for a landing during a Sentry Eagle exercise in 1988. This 114th-sponsored event, a large-scale, composite force employment exercise similar to a Red Flag exercise, took place for the first time in 1986. (Courtesy of Ron Olsen.)

The arrival of Santa Claus always excites children, as seen in the crowd around the Kingsley F-4 crew ladder in this 1980s picture. S.M.Sgt. Doug Riese occupies the front seat, and the jolly backseater is M.Sgt. Bob Dunn. This tradition was a popular opener for the annual children's Christmas party. It began during the F-4 years and lasted through the F-16 era and into the F-15 period until at least 2007.

Weapons loaders with the 142nd CAMS go through their paces at a missile trailer and prepare to load weapons onto a smartly painted 123rd FIS F-4C at the William Tell meet in 1986. Evaluators watch closely to time and grade their performance. The three Oregon Air Guardsmen in fatigue uniforms are, from left to right, Paul Verheyden (with headband), Bob Avery, and Mark Wiebold (crew chief).

The parking ramp at Kingsley Field is filled with a wide variety of aircraft for Exercise Sentry Eagle in 1986, the first of a continuing series of ANG aerial exercises similar to the Red Flag exercises held at Nellis Air Force Base in Nevada. Shown here are a KC-135 and several F-15s, A-7s, F-16s, F/A-18s, and Canadian CF-5s.

As the Cold War ended, the 114th continued its schoolhouse training role for the pilots of ANG air defense units selected to convert to the specially-modified F-16 ADF. In March 1988, Col. Steven Harper delivered the first operational F-16B ADF to Kingsley Field. One visible air defense modification was the spotlight on the nose just aft of the radome, used for visually identifying aircraft at night.

The support aircraft that followed the ORANG's venerable C-131 was the Lockheed C-130A Hercules. It was used for the usual variety of support tasks and included shuttling alert aircrew back and forth between Portland and Kingsley Field for OLAD operations. Although the 142nd's F-4s had lost their colorful Redhawk in the change from ADC Gray to the subdued Hill Gray paint scheme, this C-130A adopted the ADC Gray and Redhawk.

The ORANG has occasionally provided urgent humanitarian assistance to citizens in need. Here, crew chief Kenneth Coats takes a packet of anti-snakebite serum from pilot Jack Fisher and weapons system officer Steve Allison in a c. 1989 photograph. Portland had run out of the serum and sent this alert aircraft to Klamath Falls to quickly bring the serum to Portland.

In February 1990, the 142nd Civil Engineer Squadron (CES) deployed to Jamaica to help rebuild five preschools damaged during a hurricane that previous September. They also brought basic school supplies for over 200 children, donations from Fred Meyers and City Liquidators. Here, American ambassador Glen Holden (originally from Lake Oswego, Oregon) holds the CES sign amidst a group of villagers and Oregon Air Guardsmen. Many children happily hold "Freddy" bears.

The ORANG directly witnessed the Cold War's thawing when Redhawk F-15s escorted Soviet fighter aircraft across American skies in June 1990. Here, a trio of 142nd FIG Eagles begins escorting a pair of white-nosed Soviet Su-27 Flanker fighters as Canadian CF-18 Hornets hand over escort duties. It was the first time Soviet fighter jets flew across America, en route to an air show in Oklahoma City.

Six

1990s

Flying with Teenagers

With the Cold War's end, some wondered whether the air defense mission was still relevant. Strange things were seen, such as the ORANG's escort in June 1990 of Soviet Su-27 Flanker fighters across US airspace en route to participate in an Oklahoma air show.

In a reflection of a changing world, ORANG ground formations began participating in expeditionary operations overseas. In November 1994, the 142nd Medical Squadron deployed to Honduras and provided medical care to 3,000 impoverished villagers.

In March 1996, the 142nd Fighter Wing (FW) deployed F-15s to Iceland for alert duty while it maintained home-base alert. The ORANG also began sending jets for counter-drug alert duty in Panama. In June 1996, responsibility for Kingsley Field transferred from the 142nd FW to the ORANG's new 173rd FW.

Even with an increased operations tempo, the post–Cold War peace dividend was still being paid for in force reductions. In September 1996, the ORANG's 104th Air Control Squadron inactivated.

The year 1998 was another busy one. In February 1998, the 173rd FW converted to the F-15 Eagle and continued schoolhouse duties for the strategic air defense community.

Overseas deployments continued. In March 1998, the 142nd FW deployed to Turkey, flying F-15s to enforce the no-fly zone (NFZ) over northern Iraq. The same month, the 270th Air Traffic Control Squadron deployed from Kingsley Field to Hungary for Balkans peacekeeping operations. May 1998 saw the 116th Air Control Squadron deploy to Italy in support of the same.

As the decade closed, the ORANG continued to provide the principle air defense of the Pacific Northwest and simultaneously conducted a wide variety of community projects and expeditionary and humanitarian assistance missions in the turbulent post–Cold War environment. These included deployments to Saudi Arabia in 2000 to patrol the NFZ over southern Iraq and several trips to Panama in May 1999. ORANG F-15 pilots flew some of the last counter-drug missions from Howard Air Force Base in Panama before the base was closed. Oregon Air Guardsmen also deployed to places like Belize, Macedonia, South Korea, Curaçao, Denmark, Germany, Guam, Kuwait, Spain, and the United Kingdom, among others.

In September 1991, the ORANG celebrated its 50th anniversary with a big commemoration in conjunction with a 123rd Observation Squadron reunion, a 123rd World War II memorial, and Memorial Park dedications. The new park included a garden setting, flagpole, memorials, and permanent static display of F-101B and F-4C aircraft. The dedication included ORANG veterans, patriotic music, a 21-gun salute, and an F-15 flyover in the missing man formation.

The Memorial Park dedication also featured a new memorial to Oregon's fallen Air Guardsmen. Here, Mary Clark views the memorial that honored her husband, Lt. Col. Gerald Clark, lost in September 1978, and the names of 16 others. The list of names is longer now as Air Guardsmen and women continue to faithfully serve.

When the 142nd FIG converted to the F-15 in 1989, it also moved its alert detachment (which became Detachment 1) from Kingsley Field up to McChord Air Force Base in Washington. Here, a Redhawk F-15 prepares to depart the alert barn at McChord, a facility formerly occupied by interceptors from the "Green Dragons" of the active-duty 318th FIS. Detachment 1 maintained alert at McChord through September 1993, when defense cuts closed operations.

In May 1992, members of the 142nd Civil Engineering Squadron deployed to a tactical communications and navigation site atop a 4,600-foot-tall mountain in Honduras. There, they built a dining hall, barracks, and shower facility for the remote site during their annual two-week training.

The Fairchild C-26 Metroliner was the last operational support aircraft assigned to the ORANG. It joined the ORANG at Portland in August 1990 and flew for several years in the 1990s before it was removed from Oregon's inventory. This picture was taken in September 1990 at Portland ANG Base. (Courtesy of Paul Carter.)

In May 1994, 1st Lt. Michelle Carson became the first female pilot assigned to the ORANG. An active-duty AF pilot assigned to the 142nd Fighter Group to fly the C-26 for a three-year tour, she is seen here in the Metroliner's right seat.

A 114th TFTS F-16B from Kingsley Field flies past scenic Mount Thielsen and Diamond Lake in southern Oregon. In 1992, the squadron was redesignated as a fighter squadron, and it continued to fly the F-16 until it changed to the F-15 in 1998.

In February 1996, the Columbia River again threatened Portland Air Base. Operational aircraft deployed to McChord Air Force Base in Washington and quickly reset for alert operations. Nonoperational aircraft were towed to higher ground at the Colwood National Golf Club's parking lot along Columbia Boulevard in Portland and stayed until the threat of flood receded. They are shown here with some AF Reserve HH-60 rescue helicopters, fuel trucks, and assorted aerospace ground equipment.

Successive post–Cold War defense cuts continued to affect the ORANG. In September 1996, the 104th Air Control Squadron (ACS) inactivated in a bittersweet ceremony held at Coos Head ANG Station in Coos Bay, Oregon. The squadron, established in 1971 at Kingsley Field, moved to North Bend in 1981 and to Coos Head in 1988. It received two Oregon ANG and one AF Outstanding Unit awards during its service.

At the invitation of ORANG recruiters (wearing ties), former Portland Trail Blazers Kermit Washington (left) and Mychal Thompson visited the 142nd FW in February 1997. They hosted the Portland area's only NBA sports talk show on KFFX AM radio, toured the base, and spoke to personnel at the flight simulator, life support, hangar, and engine test facility. They scarcely fit into the cockpit of an F-15 fighter.

The roar of the powerful F-15 jet engines is muffled inside the engine test facility on Portland Air Base, also known as the "Hush House," in this 1997 view. The Hush House significantly reduces the noise from jet engine testing required following regular maintenance of the Eagle's Pratt & Whitney F100 afterburning turbofan power plants.

One of the first Kingsley Field F-15A Eagles rests as a static display during an air show at Naval Air Station Whidbey Island in July 1998. The first F-15 arrived at Kingsley in February 1998. A scant two weeks later, the last F-16s departed as the 173rd FW quickly transitioned to the Eagle and continued with its schoolhouse mission. (Courtesy of Paul Carter.)

In early 1998, the 142nd FW deployed to Incirlik Air Base in Turkey to patrol the northern no-fly zone over Iraq. The wing rotated three groups of Air Guardsmen through the deployment in a period just before tensions with Iraq picked up again. Here, Oregon Air Guardsmen take a break for a deployment photograph opportunity under skies reminiscent of the Pacific Northwest.

In the fall of 2000, the 142nd FW deployed to Prince Sultan Air Base in Saudi Arabia and patrolled the southern no-fly zone over Iraq. These missions required great care to execute. In this picture, a Redhawk F-15 soars over the desert in a time when a virtual undeclared war was underway as Iraqi air defense units fired on coalition aircraft and, in return, coalition aircraft attacked them.

Seven

2000s

Air Defense Reprise

As the 2000s unfolded, the ORANG fulfilled repeated USAF expeditionary taskings, many to Southwest Asia, as part of the Total Force.

On September 11, 2001, the ORANG quickly responded to terrorist attacks with an increased readiness posture. Both fighter wings and the 116th ACS participated in the national military call to homeland defense.

ORANG personnel provided national humanitarian aid in the wakes of Hurricanes Katrina and Rita and to Oregonians affected by the 2007 floods in Vernonia.

In William Tell's 50th Anniversary competition in 2004, the 142nd FW was first in maintenance, element attack, and gun categories. This demonstrated Oregon's long history of outstanding performance and mission readiness.

ORANG's transition to the ultimate F-15 variant, the "Golden Eagle," began in April 2010 when the first two aircraft arrived at Portland for operations with the 142nd FW.

In October 2010, the Evergreen Aviation and Space Museum feted the ORANG's founders when it inducted the 123rd Observation Squadron into the museum's Hall of Honor.

Also, in October 2010, the 142nd FW deployed to the United Arab Emirates' Gulf Air Warfare Center for a Red Flag–like exercise with Gulf and allied nations.

As the ORANG's eighth decade begins, it continues Aerospace Control Alert (ACA) operations. Its steady alert tempo is punctuated by expeditionary taskings, many in the form of individual Air Guardsmen, and sometimes as a unit.

On April 15, 2011, the 142nd FW hosted the ORANG's 70th anniversary commemoration at Portland Air Base. It was highlighted by the participation of seven of the eight surviving original 123rd Observation Squadron members. Some Air Guardsmen were unable to participate in the commemoration, as the ORANG deployed the 116th ACS and over 80 personnel to Southwest Asia in March 2011.

As this book goes to press, the ORANG's minutemen and women maintain their nonstop ACA vigil in the Pacific Northwest, train all American F-15 pilots, provide and air battle management specialized battlefield airman capabilities, and ensure readiness to fulfill additional tasks as directed. Oregon's citizen airmen are a vital part of today's Total Force and serve their community, state, and nation proudly.

The ORANG's 173rd FW deployed to Minsk-Mazowiecki Air Base in Poland for an inter-operability training exercise with a key NATO ally in May 2001. Adjacent to a Polish AF MIG-29UB fighter-trainer, from left to right are Brig. Gen. James Cunningham (HQ ORANG chief of staff), maj dypl. pil. (Maj.) Krzysztof Rosa (1st Tactical Squadron commander), and Maj. Gen. Alexander Burgin (adjutant general of the Oregon National Guard).

Col. Garry Dean was the ORANG's first senior leader of African heritage to hold high command positions when he became the 142nd FW commander in January 2001. He first joined the ORANG in 1990, after service on active duty and with the Georgia ANG. He later became the ORANG commander, was promoted to major general, and served as the first Air Force commander before his latest assignment to NATO.

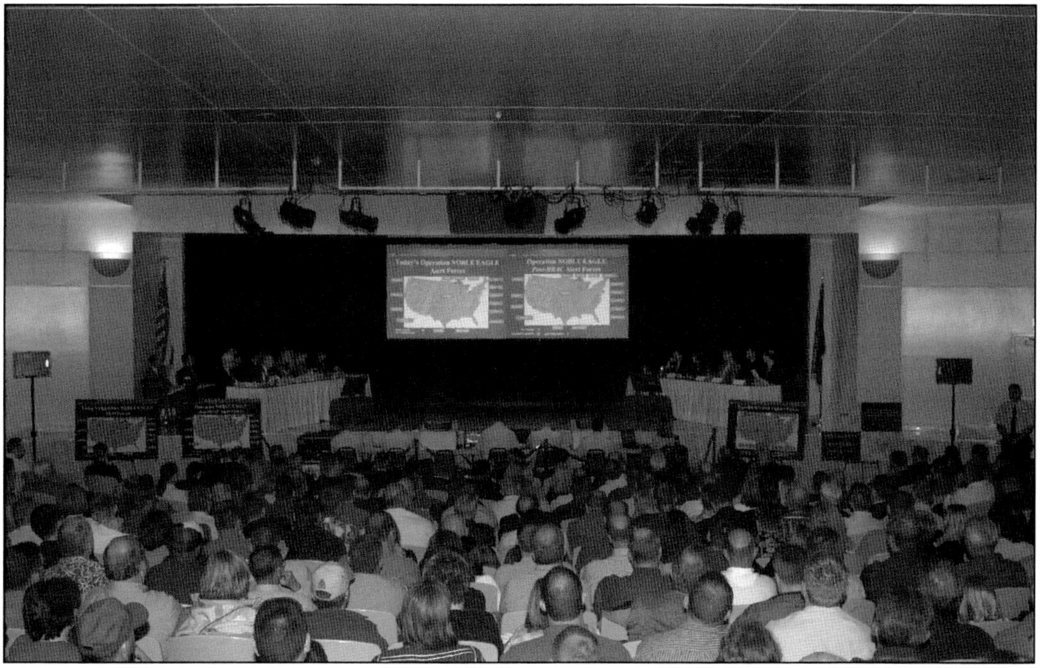

When the Defense Department announced its intent to close down all military flying operations at Portland Air Base in 2005, the Congressional Base Realignment and Closure Commission came to Portland to review the recommendation. State and regional leaders articulated a compelling case for retaining the military aviation mission at the Northwest regional hearing held in Portland in June 2005. The ORANG F-15 alert mission was ultimately retained.

Fire trucks with water cannons greeted the arrival of the first F-15Cs to Portland in May 2007. Col. Steven Gregg, 142nd FW commander, and Lt. Col. Steve Beauchamp brought this newer version of the F-15 to Portland from Kadena Air Base in Okinawa to commence an upgrade from the F-15A.

The ORANG returned to an old stomping ground in 2009 when base improvements necessitated the 173rd FW's temporary relocation from Kingsley Field to Gowen Field, Idaho. Here, a 173rd FW Eagle takes off on a routine training mission. The ORANG deployed to Gowen Field for summer training several times during the 1950s. (Courtesy of 173rd FW Public Affairs.)

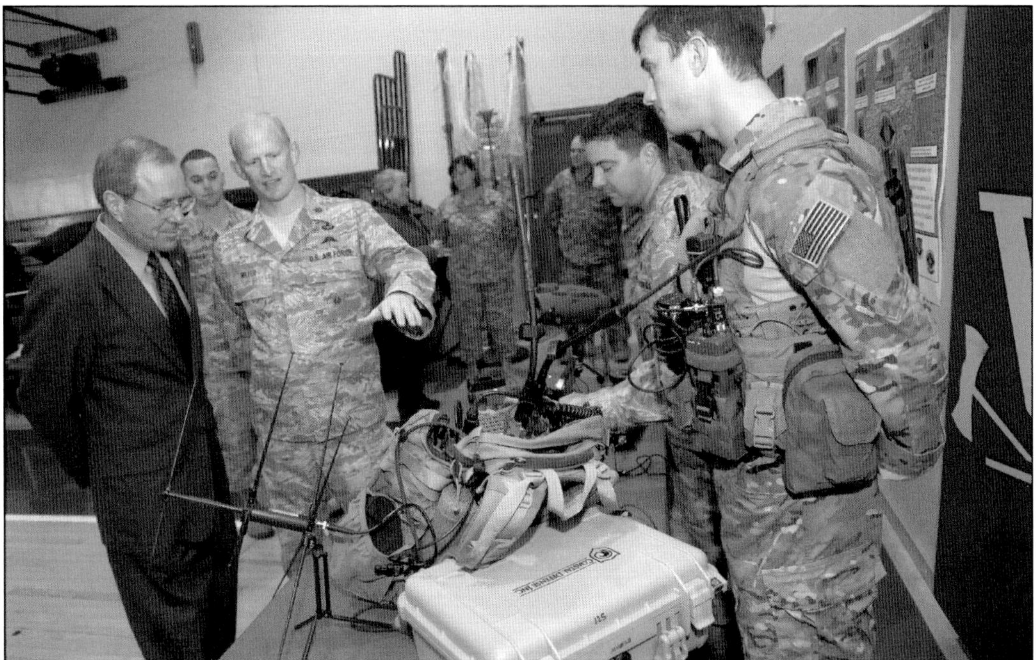

Oregon governor Ted Kulongoski received a briefing from ORANG major Jake Miller, commander of the 125th Special Tactics Squadron, on the squadron's communication equipment at Vernonia High School in Vernonia, Oregon, during a ground-breaking ceremony for a new school and community center in December 2010. The squadron, along with other Oregon National Guard elements, responded to the flooding in Vernonia in 2007 and helped rescue many residents. (US Air Force photograph by T.Sgt. John Hughel; courtesy of Oregon National Guard Public Affairs.)

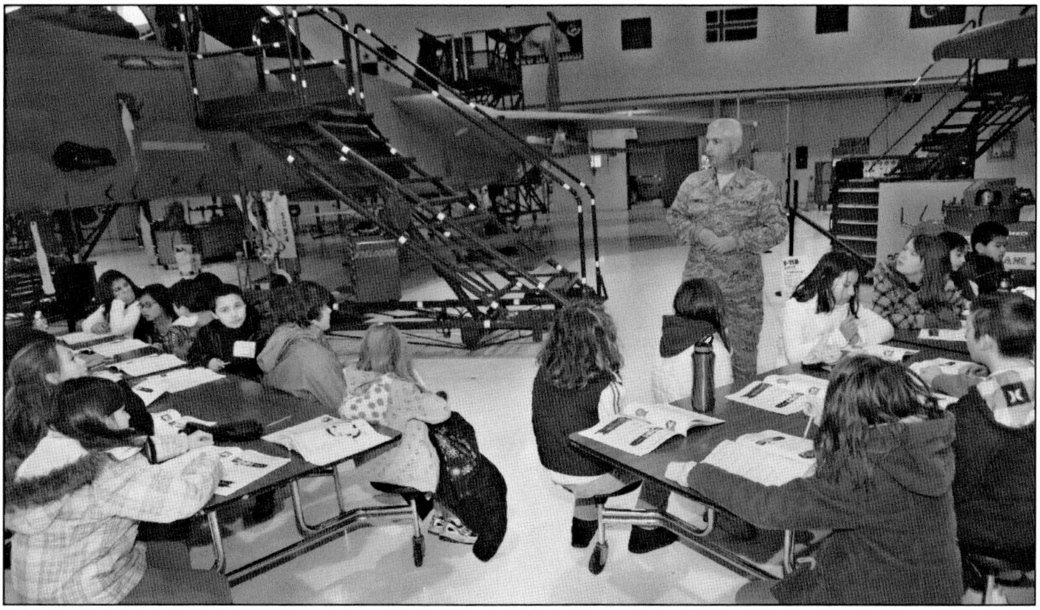

Both Portland Air Base and Kingsley Field host the Defense Department–sponsored STARBASE educational program, which helps local communities reinforce science, technology, engineering, and math learning with hands-on opportunities. In January 2011, S.M.Sgt. Stan Durfee of the ORANG 142nd Aircraft Maintenance Squadron spoke during a base tour to fifth-graders from Woodstock Elementary School in Portland. (US Air Force photograph by T.Sgt. John Hughel; courtesy of 142nd Fighter Wing Public Affairs.)

Retired C.M.Sgt. Jack Klein (left) and A1c. Elliot Gile participated in a memorial wreath ceremony during the ORANG's 70th anniversary celebration at Portland ANG Base on April 15, 2011. Oregon National Guard senior leaders stand behind them. Gile, a 142nd FW crew chief, was the ORANG's newest member, while Klein was the ORANG's first recruiter and served as a radar operator with the 142nd Aircraft Control and Warning Squadron. (US Air Force photograph by M.Sgt. Jon Dyer; courtesy of 142nd Fighter Wing Public Affairs.)

Pioneers of today's ORANG from the 123rd Observation Squadron gathered for a photograph together after the ORANG's 70th-anniversary celebration held at Portland ANG Base on April 15, 2011. From left to right are original members Ben Olbrich, Fred Parish, John Pear, Glen Curry, John Donis, and Fred Hill. (US Air Force photograph by T.Sgt. John Hughel; courtesy of 142nd Fighter Wing Public Affairs.)

Camp Rosenbaum continues to provide Oregon youth with a wholesome summer recreation opportunity. Youth counselor Myriam Demenzas of the Portland Housing Authority, a youth mentor at the camp for more than five years, shares a laugh with a young camper during the July 2011 encampment. (US Air Force photograph by T.Sgt. John Hughel; courtesy of 142nd Fighter Wing Public Affairs.)

Air Guardsmen of the 116th Air Control Squadron took part in a demobilization ceremony in July 2011 after a four-month deployment to Southwest Asia. The ceremony was held in the Rosenbaum Hangar at Portland ANG Base, which provides the Oregon National Guard a rainy weather shelter option for such events to take place. (US Air Force photograph by T.Sgt. John Hughel; courtesy of 142nd Fighter Wing Public Affairs.)

As part of her responsibilities to engage with the citizens of Oregon, Caroline McGowan, Miss Oregon 2011, visited Portland ANG Base and met with Air Guardsmen in August 2011. She was crowned Miss Oregon on July 1, 2011. Here, she stands with base firefighters. From left to right are Morgan Hall, Jon Hayes, Miss Oregon, Mark Scheehean, M.Sgt. Mike Wou, and Mark Hernandez. (US Air Force photograph by S.Sgt. Aaron Perkins; courtesy of 142nd Fighter Wing Public Affairs.)

Chief of the National Guard Bureau Gen. Craig McKinley visited Port of Portland offices at Portland International Airport in September 2011. He thanked port representatives for their 60 years of partnership with the Oregon Air National Guard. From left to right are General McKinley, Maj. Gen. Raymond Rees (Oregon's adjutant general), Steven Schreiber (director of aviation), and Paul Rosenbaum (port commission treasurer). (US Air Force photograph by T.Sgt. John Hughel; courtesy of 142nd Fighter Wing Public Affairs.)

An F-15 of the ORANG's 142nd Fighter Wing thunders into the Northwest skies during the June 2006 Operational Readiness Inspection from Air Combat Command. The ORANG maintains a high state of readiness in order to provide continuous ACA capability. As they did when they started in 1941, Oregon's citizen airmen stand ready today to answer the call to duty. (US Air Force photograph by T.Sgt. John Hughel; courtesy of 142nd Fighter Wing Public Affairs.)

BIBLIOGRAPHY

25th Air Defense Division, 1953–1954. Baton Rouge, LA: Army and Navy Publishing Company, 1953.

A Brief History of the 160th Aircraft Control & Warning Group in the Alaskan Theater of Operations, May 1951–February 1953. Camp Withycombe, OR: Oregon Military Department and Oregon Military Museum, 1998.

Deur, John M. *William Tell 1984.* Vista, CA: Aeolus Publishing Limited, 1986.

Ellis, T.Sgt. Lori, ed. *Oregon Air National Guard, 1941–1991: A Commemorative History.* Dallas, TX: Taylor Publishing Company, 1990.

Filson, Leslie. *Air War Over America: Sept. 11 Alters Face of Air Defense Mission.* Tyndall AFB, FL: Headquarters, 1st Air Force, 2003.

Gross, Charles J. *Prelude to the Total Force: The Air National Guard, 1943–1969.* Washington, DC: Office of Air Force History, 1985.

Hellickson, Gene. *Mobile Military Radar.* www.mobileradar.org/ (Accessed October 25, 2011.)

Isham, Marty and David R. McClaren. *Northrop F-89 Scorpion: A Photo Chronicle.* Atglen, PA: Schiffer Military/Aviation History, 1996.

Knack, Marcele Size. *Post–World War II Fighters, 1945–1973.* Washington, DC: Office of Air Force History, 1986

Schaffel, Kenneth. *The Emerging Shield: The Air Force and the Evolution of Continental Air Defense, 1945–1960.* Washington, DC: Office of Air Force History, 1991.